LANDING YOUR DREAM JOB

Start Your Career *Ahead* of the Competition

"A very informative, useful and concise guide. I will definitely be applying the tips mentioned in this book when looking for jobs in the future."
Mai Ngo
Student at the University of New South Wales, 2010

TOBY MARSHALL

Praise for Toby Marshall's Previous Careers and Recruitment Book

"Innovative and insightful – a great resource for up and coming professionals to boost their career."

Tim Dein,
President NSW AHRI Council (Australian Human Resources Institute)

"Frank, often entertaining and extremely practical –absolute gold! This is an excellent resource without the ego – well worth a read."

Lesley Horsburgh,
Managing Editor of 'Recruitment EXTRA'

"Easy to read, practical advice."

Melanie Laing,
Asia Pacific Director HR, Unisys

"A refreshingly candid account...results in some powerful insights. A must read for anyone and everyone involved in business today."

Elinor Crossing,
Talent Management Consultant

"Toby's best selling book Get a Better Job / Get Great People is filled with refreshing and unique insights into the recruitment industry."

Lisa Messenger,
Group Managing Director at The Messenger Group

"After 39 years in HR I've found an expert who truly understands recruitment. In Toby's engrossing book, he speaks about inefficient practices that cost employers money and applicants their dignity. He cares about both and has created a process for leading organisations to find the best people without wasting money."

Rodney Gray,
Principal of Employee Communication & Surveys

Praise for Toby Marshall's Recruitment & Careers Advice

"Toby has given me invaluable careers guidance for almost two years. He has no hesitation in giving up his time and his advice. I would highly recommend Toby for those seeking to build a better, more satisfying career."

Lara Ette,
Trading & Professional Counteparty Sales, ANZ Investment Bank

"Toby has a way of finding out exactly what is required – from a recruiter's and a recruitee's point of view. He has a unique way of approaching recruitment that results in 'best fits', and he understands the market clearly."

Sharonne Phillips,
Speaker, consultant and author

"Toby Marshall is the spearhead of the recruitment revolution. Toby has the creativity, vision and organisational skills that are changing the way leading organisations recruit and retain their staff. His approach is unique but his results are universal. If you need the right people for the right job then Toby's your man."

Nils Vesk,
Professional Designer & Director at Nils Vesk Pty. Ltd.

"Toby is a breath of fresh air in the recruitment industry. He has a fine mind and writes excellent and readable publications. He is generous in sharing his knowledge and experience in order to make a better world for us all."

Wayne Sullivan,
CEO at Marwick & Stimson

"Useful advice – not the usual bulldust!"
(last word in this quote required editing)

Annie de Botton,
HR Manager Wealth and Asset Management, Perpetual

"This book is accessible and may very well counteract our society's overemphasis on tertiary qualifications. You'll find yourself unravelling many myths about working in the real world, a process crucial to making it big out there."
Ann Pham, student at the University of New South Wales, 2010.

About the Author and Contributors...

Author/Grey Guru:

Toby Marshall

Toby Marshall has had extensive experience within the recruitment industry. Acting as the Director of Abacus Recruitment Solutions, Toby learnt what employers look for in potential job candidates and has chosen to pass this information on to young people, hoping to steer them in the right direction of landing their dream job.

Principal of the small business marketing company, Lead Creation Pty Ltd., Toby and his young team – including university undergraduates and interns – strive to improve online marketing strategies for small businesses, targeting their niche markets to attract attention from both existing and prospective clients.

Young Writers:

Alongside Toby, a team of young writers contributed a lot of effort to the creation of this book. Ellie McDonald, Melanie Wagner and Carli Alman have each worked as Copywriting interns and staff with Toby at Abacus Recruitment and his new business Lead Creation whilst completing their undergraduate degrees at university.

Young Recruiters:

Caroline Maroon, Alyse Cassoniti, Samantha Rego and Sean Bailey are the young recruiters who also offered their help in the making of Toby's book. You'll see some of their anecdotes throughout this book. This dedicated group of Human Resources interns and staff, like the Lead Creation Copywriters, balanced working with Toby at Lead Creation and attending university.

Thanks to the Team

This is a wide ranging book, covering a vast amount of information regarding a person's first steps into ascertaining their dream job. Numerous young staff and interns contributed their expertise and hard work to make this in-depth book possible. A big thank you for all your help and passion.

Chief Editor and Copywriter: Ellie McDonald

Writing Coordinator and Copywriter: Melanie Wagner

The team:

Carli Alman – Copywriter

Belinda Terlato – Copywriter

Storay Mangal – Copywriter

Valentine Gunadharma – Graphic Designer

Peter Zhu – Cartoonist

Lincoln Smith – Marketing

Caroline Maroon – Human Resources

Sean Bailey – Human Resources

Samantha Rego – Human Resources

Alyse Cassaniti – Human Resources

Emilie Donnell – Administration and Editing

It is also worth noting that this book was written in Australia, however, the ideas and suggestions are universal and can be applied to any country. See back of book for a glossary of Australian terms.

Contents

Contents

Chapter 1: Education, Choices and Getting Your Parents On-Board

So, how great do I have to be to get a DREAM job?

Research shows that natural talent is not the key to great future success—thank god! The secret of success is simple: practice and hard work, as well as a passion for what you are doing—see sidenote***.

***A sidenote from the 'Grey Guru'

"We all know that Tiger Woods is the world's greatest golfer. In an earlier edition of this book, we talked about how much practice and hard work he had put in to become as successful as he is today. By the age of 15, he had put in as much practice as the average golf tour professional has by the age of 30.

Despite the 'hard work' Woods put into his tragic personal life in the last year, this world-renowned sports star certainly proved that regular practice is vital in getting the career you want. Apply this to landing your dream job: your chosen endeavour is far more important than getting a degree, particularly when it's the wrong degree (See Ch. 2)."

So I don't have to be a genius with a UAI or ATAR of 99.95, then?

You certainly do not. The evidence is overwhelming—it really is practice that makes perfect, but not just <u>any</u> practice. 'Deliberate practice', breaking down a process (such as Tiger Woods' backswing) into its components, and then repeating them over and over again, aiming for improvement each time. You must set **specific, measurable, achievable goals.** Then, you **observe the results, making adjustments to your technique** as you go. Raw talent or genius has little to do with it.

This type of practice can be difficult and at times, boring. **You should focus on practical tasks that need to be mastered—not theory and abstractions.** If you want to know more about how to practice, be sure to check out this great article from *Fortune Magazine:*

http://money.cnn.com/magazines/fortune/fortune_archive/2006/10/30/8391794/index.htm

How you can be the Champion of the Office...

Experts are now applying insights from sports performance to the world of business and the professions. It's the same old story— the people who succeed are the ones who push themselves that little bit harder each day, pay attention to feedback, and don't assume that learning stops when you graduate from university.

Most of us aren't going to become professional golfers, but all of us are going to get a job.

The right kind of practice at work has the potential to make or break your career. It will make the difference between a rewarding, satisfying job where you really use your skills, and a role where you're set up to fail.

But our education system, our corporate culture, and our society as a whole doesn't get it yet. They get you to study and practice really hard, learning things that will probably be irrelevant to your future success. How so? We send almost all of you off to university, regardless of whether it's the right path for you or not. You continue your studies until the age of 21 or 23, learning things you'll never use.

You're there for so long that by the time you graduate you've forgotten about 95% of what you've learnt. More research has been done on learning in the past 20 years than in the rest of human history, and it consistently shows that about 70% of learning is through experience, 20% is learning from others, and only 10% is through formal study.

It's quite obvious when you think about it. You attend a half-day training program and start using what you've learnt the next day. If you go on using it, you've embedded a new skill. This is *'just in time'* learning and it works.

Why taking on a degree you're not 100% sure about can often be a waste of time....

You'd think course content would be up-to-date and reflect what's going on in the real world. However, it's not the case.

Your lecturers don't work at the core of the industry where knowledge and new skills are developed every day, month, and year. They work in the classroom.

Combine this with:

95% of information you learn at university is forgotten before you start working in your desired field. Knowledge is being created and disseminated faster than ever before. Plus narrow, specialised jobs in different professions are growing. If this doesn't make you think twice about doing a five-year degree, nothing will.

The Did You Know 3.0 video is a really great source of information that tells you more about the rapidly changing job market, and may help you to find your place in it, so be sure to have a look at it:

http://www.youtube.com/watch?v=jpEnFwiqdx8&feature=fvst

Professor of Education at the University of Sydney, Geoffrey Sherington, and author of 'School Choice' states, *"people choose a career, not a course"*. This is a huge risk because very few people know what that career actually involves (see Ch. 2).

Although, sometimes a university degree is essential as society has deemed it so. For example, no Law degree, no career in law— see sidenote***.

***A sidenote from the 'Grey Guru'

"My business is called Lead Creation and we use New Media marketing to generate leads for small to medium sized businesses (http://www.leadcreation.com.au/). Now, there are 6 core elements or components that make up a modern marketing system.

Not one of the 15 undergraduate marketing students who have worked with us in the last 12 months as interns have studied or been exposed to more than one or two of them in uni— and usually that was just one lecture. One core component is Google Pay Per Click Ads, the fastest growing advertising marketing in the world—and in Australia it is growing 25% a year even after the recession. Universities virtually ignore it.

It's scary that you can choose to study something technical or work-focused like Marketing or Communication, thinking that it will advance your career. Most of what you learn is pretty worthless and will be forgotten before you graduate."

To put it bluntly, university is going to fill your head with the theoretical and the abstract, leaving out the stuff that's actually important. Go to uni to learn how to reason, think and explore life. Just don't expect it to help much with your career beyond the required piece of paper.

Don't believe us?

The Big 4 Accounting Firms in Sydney have to put their new graduate recruits through a lot of on-the-job training and a number of training programs so that they can do the job that they were hired for. That's just to teach them the very basics! This tells us two things:

1. Universities are failing to design practical, relevant courses

2. You don't need 3 years of study to become an accountant—they can teach you enough to get you started in 3 months!

It hasn't always been this way. Forty years ago, 77% of young people left school before their final year to go straight into the workforce. Today, it's less than 15%. In many of the professions, including Accounting and Law, you used to primarily learn on the job. These days, without a tertiary degree you simply won't get hired—see sidenote***.

*** A sidenote from the 'Grey Guru'

"I studied Accounting at university, and the course content was horrifyingly outdated and irrelevant. After studying for 2 years, I got a summer job with a small accounting practice. It took me 2 days to perform a bank reconciliation, whereas the 18-year-old school leaver, who had had 6 months work experience, did it in 2 hours. Unsurprisingly, they let me go after a week.

So, why do companies want their employees to have degrees?

In some cases, it is a requirement issued by an industry association. The degree provides evidence that the student can apply him or herself and be persistent.

But I want to be a Photographer!

A common theme among young people can be seen within their career aspirations, listing professions like becoming a photographer, a designer, an artist, a novelist, or an actor. Their parents smile indulgently, and warn them that they'll be competing for work in a heavily popular field. Well, someone has to succeed at it. Why not you? See sidenote ***.

*** A sidenote from the 'Grey Guru'

"It stunned me a few years ago when my daughter was in Year 10, preparing for work experience. Within her year group of 105 girls, 70 wanted to do their work experience in design. Jaw-dropping. For every designer we need at least a few hundred people to buy their designs. If two-thirds of young women go off to work as a designer, who will buy their products?

Clearly, there's not enough work. The sad part is that they wasted the opportunity to learn about a different job that <u>could</u> provide a dream career."

It's understandable that many young people want to be a photographer or designer. These jobs are glamorous and interesting, and a <u>few</u> highly paid people who have achieved fame in these fields now lead very exciting lives. What you may not know is that those people usually worked incredibly hard from a very young age. They were completely focused on their craft, to the point of obsession, and made sacrifices to get where they are today.

It's easy to say you want to be a photographer, but you have to be honest with yourself about your motives, and how hard you are prepared to work to make it happen. How many people planning to study photography have actually spent hours <u>every</u> day taking photographs, long before they started studying and had to turn in assignments? Not just taking photographs, but constantly thinking about angles and compositions as they walk down the street, seeing their life through the lens of a camera.

Truly great people, in any field, practice constantly—7 days a week, 365 days a year. Very few of us have the willpower and dedication to match that. And why should we! That kind of life is not for everyone. Quite frankly, it doesn't sound like that much fun, does it?

Two words of advice to people dreaming of working in photography or design, or any other high demand industry that promises glory but pays appalling wages to the many who try to achieve it: <u>Prove yourself</u>. Prove how badly you want it, and how much work you are prepared to put in before you start a long and expensive university degree or diploma course that leads you absolutely nowhere.

Get the X Factor

Most of us aren't geniuses, sporting legends, or world-renowned musicians. We don't need to be! We all have the very real potential to achieve greatness in our lives—the contentment and fulfilment of being great at whatever it is we do, and reaping the rewards of our work. You may not be the next Warren Buffet and dominate the global investment industry, but you could be a well-regarded fund manager.

Now, we could argue forever about whether Tiger Woods would have reached the heights in his professional career that he has without all the practice and dedication. Chances are that with his genes, at the very least he still would have been a reasonably good tour professional, earning a couple of hundred thousand a year. But the fact is people who are willing to put in the time and hard work have a <u>massive advantage</u> over those who don't.

The research doesn't tell us why it is that some people have such an unstoppable will to succeed, but that doesn't really matter. For *you* to have a great, satisfying, and rewarding career, you just need to work a little bit harder than the vast majority of people who read books like this, and never get around to putting it into practice. You need to focus, keep your eyes on the prize, and get a little bit better every day. All that practice adds up, and the time you take now will pay dividends later on.

The Grey Guru's 6 Best Career Tips

Start practicing early, worry less about the degree, and more about getting practical experience. Once you find out what you're really good at and what you enjoy, then you can really get down to studying. Remember, what makes a dream job is different for everyone—one size doesn't fit all.

Here are some tips to help get you started:

Read this book! We've done the hard work for you. Just sit back, relax and take it in

Get relevant work experience. All students need to work part-time to earn money, so why not make your job useful as well? Employers need and want experience, and it's the best way to get your foot in the door

Ignore what they teach you at uni. By all means go, and get your passport (i.e. your degree), but remember, at the end of the day it's just a piece of paper. Don't kill yourself trying to get top marks, because it doesn't count for much in the real world. Study less, and use that time to get a part-time job or internship where you can learn something really useful

Learn a 'young person' skill. If you excel in one of the things listed below, it will open doors and make companies want to interview you and give you part-time work. This could also lead to being hired once you graduate. Try learning Excel, SEO [1], social networking: LinkedIn, Facebook, Twitter, etc. Syncing a mobile phone, or PC productivity improvements

<u>Ignore your parents or career advisor</u>, but pretend not to, unless they've read this book and agree with the approach

<u>Start networking early</u>. Get involved in a team sport, and make sure you have friends from a broad range of social and ethnic groups. Get some good Career Buddies
(see Ch. 4)

Most importantly, do what you love with energy and passion. Don't choose a career just for the money because chances are you'll end up feeling miserable.

Above all, learn every day! Learn 'just in time', and just enough. <u>Use</u> your knowledge and apply it, because that's the only way you'll really learn.

Four Extra Tips for Migrant Kids

If you come from a non-English speaking background, you have certain advantages—you're bilingual, and there's better food at home! However, you also have to make sure you don't get disadvantaged in the job market:

---

[1] Don't know what it is? It's worth looking up as it's a new industry that hadn't been dreamt of just 10 years ago.

1. If you learnt English recently and it's not quite perfect, get a friend to review your cover letters and resumes. It's critical that the words and the grammar are absolutely perfect.

2. Practice your <u>spoken</u> English and your business English. There are a number of courses that help you with this, and the best source that we recommend is the Performance English website:

    http://www.performanceenglish.com.au/home.html

3. Play an 'Anglo' team sport. Who cares how bad you are at it! There are many sports, like touch football, basketball, or netball that people of all sizes and all abilities can play. Why an Anglo sport? Well it's a way to grow your networks and it's a way to become more in tune with the culture you're now living in—and that is vital for finding a great job (see Ch. 4).

4. Study Anglo body language. Ask your friends if your body language is different. It's a subtle detail, but it can be very important in making people feel comfortable around you and employers aren't going to hire someone they're not comfortable with.

This is not about making everyone the same, or saying that Anglo culture is better. But this is the dominant system that you'll be working in, and you need to know how to work in it.

When you've got the job, you can be as different as you like (as long as you do a good job).

An Open Letter to Parents from The Grey Guru:

Your child has put this book in your hands because they take their future seriously. We know you do as well and that you passionately want them to do well. So, don't just regurgitate the advice you were given all those years ago—the world has changed.

As parents, we have become confused when it comes to careers and education. We can put it down to a couple of powerful human emotions: status anxiety and wanting the best for our kids and assuming that this means going to university—any course at university, the 'best' that the marks allow.

So, what do I mean by status anxiety? For example, we know that plumbers often build very successful businesses and make a lot of money. But not many kids grow up dreaming of the glamorous life of a plumber—it's not a very high-status job. Even in Australia, snobbery is everywhere. Put a successful man in a certain environment (say, an expensive ski resort) and watch them stare at the ground when you ask what they do for a living—"Oh, I'm just a tradie", he mumbles. This is madness! Then again, the 'impoverished gentleman' has been a hallmark of Anglo-Saxon society for centuries: "I may be poor, but at least I don't get my hands dirty!".

Status anxiety is irrational and should have no place in our society. Some of the happiest people I know are 'tradies'. These people have a great time on the job, an outdoors lifestyle, and couldn't care less about academic snobbery.

A classic example of this is nursing. Nursing got turned into a university degree, raising its status, and attracting smarter students. However, when these students graduated, they became frustrated—they had all this knowledge and education, and wanted more responsibility. However, doctors resisted them at every turn. The education system took a practical trade that was travelling just fine, and misguidedly attempted to 'improve' it.

They failed dismally. Hopefully doctors will become increasingly open to allowing nurses to do more of the things they were always qualified to do, even before they had a degree.

Wanting the Best for Your Kids Could be Your Worst Mistake...

How is it a bad thing if we want our kids to do well, and get into a university course—the highest that their school marks allow?

Lisa Pryor was one of these students; a high achiever with a perfect UAI upon graduating. She found herself being pushed into a Law degree at Sydney University, despite having no previous interest in the subject. After 5 years of study, she ended up going into journalism instead:

> *'This is the ridiculous logic of university entrance: wasting marks is a sin. Why study Psychology when you can study Law? Why do Science when you could do Medicine? It is something like the logic of frequent flyer points: why fly economy to Tahiti when you have enough miles to take you first class all the way to Kazakhstan? Whether you would prefer a holiday in Tahiti is beside the point.'[2]*

Speaking of ridiculous, in 2009 the Communication and Media Studies course at Sydney University required a UAI of 98.45. Our top students are fighting to get into a course that provides very tenuous career opportunities in one of the most competitive industries there is. I'm not saying you shouldn't follow your passion, but you have to question the ethics of encouraging students to spend 3 years on a course that doesn't prepare them for the practicalities of working in this industry, in which the odds of finding a good, well-remunerated job are overwhelmingly stacked against them.

---

[2] Lisa Pryor, *The Pinstriped Prison*, Macmillan, 2008, p.11.

Take Accounting for example—high status degree, good reputation, and excellent future job prospects. So what's wrong with that? Well, Accounting is not for everyone, not even people with a 99.9 UAI. Too many graduates reach the finish line, land a job at a Big Four firm, get a great starting salary, only to realize that what they're doing is quite boring. Do you really want your child to study something for 4 or 5 years, only to discover that they hate it?

The UAI, or the newly implemented ATAR, purely reflects supply and demand. It is absolutely no indication of the quality of the course, future career prospects, or if it is the right course for your child. The sad fact is that the majority of students are not choosing courses like Communication and Media Studies with their eyes open. As parents, we have to be supportive of our children, and encourage them to develop their talents. Life is not all about making money, but everyone deserves a chance at a viable and satisfying career. It's our job to give them a reality check.

What to tell your kids before they choose their 'trade'...

Now, I've heard all the arguments about how university teaches you to think critically, and broadens your view of the world. I absolutely agree with that. I've supported my own children in studying at university in degrees teaching them how to conduct research, structure arguments, and to write and present papers. Although, I have strongly discouraged them to start learning a 'trade' when what they study is so often useless when they enter the world of work.

What do I mean by a trade? I'm not just talking about traditional trades like plumbing or carpentry, but whatever you do for a living—it might be Accounting, Law, Engineering, Marketing, or a thousand other things.

Many young people choose the wrong trade, but even if you have chosen the right trade, what you learn at university is simply too obsolete or too abstract—it is never going to make you an expert at that trade. All too often, these students in 4 and 5-year degree programs have gained no practical office work experience by the time they graduate. Sure, they may have done a summer internship, 'sitting in' on meetings and being babysat by overworked professionals, but do they have any real idea of whether they can do the work, or if they want to?

How Can You Ensure Your Child's Future Success?

So, how do we fix this broken-down system? The first priority is to expose young people to professional, office work before they leave school. This is where most of our top young people are going to end up, and it's crazy not to prepare them for it. This gives them the opportunity to find out what kind of work they hate, and what kind of work they're thinking about doing later in life.

By the time they reach university, your child should be continuing part-time professional work, focusing on what they are good at, and where their passion lies. At the same time they're undertaking their degree, learning research and critical skills, but their studies should take up no more than 20 hours a week. This leaves them at least two days to gain practical experience in the profession that they're likely to end up in.

By the time they graduate from university, they should be working with an employer who knows them well, is aware of what they're good at, understands the contribution they can make to the company, and where they want to go in their career. This young person, your child, is part of the team, and is already well on their way to becoming an expert at what they do.

Our current regime dictates that you 'do your time' at university, get abruptly dropped into the workforce at the end of your degree, and that's it. Game over. What we are advocating is an approach that doesn't see practical work and education as mutually exclusive. We should get on a path of lifelong learning, gaining new skills with short courses or certificates that are directly applicable to our careers.

7 Deadly parental sins

1. Doing your kid's homework, or paying tutors to. They may get the marks in the short-term, but you won't be able to hold their hands when they're in the work force.

2. Obsessing over grades. The second your child graduates, grades become completely irrelevant—certainly not worth giving them a nervous breakdown over.

3. Breaking the bank to send them to the biggest, most expensive private school. Research shows that while this might boost their marks at high school by 5% at most, by the end of their first year at uni, students from government or smaller, cheaper schools may have overtaken them.

4. Sending them to 'Cramming Colleges'. Again, this is very short-term thinking and might help your child memorise facts and figures, but it won't teach them anything.

5. Insane extra-curricular schedules. If it's not enough to get top marks, they also have to be the best violinist, the best show-jumper, and be fluent in three languages by the age of 10. They have the rest of their lives to work and achieve. Let them be kids and have a bit of fun!

6. Forcing them to follow in Mum or Dad's footsteps. Your kid is not you, and more importantly, the world has changed. Jobs are vanishing and industries are becoming completely different. What worked for you may not work for them.

7. Telling them to get a job at a big company. There's no such thing as a job-for-life anymore, and the majority of job openings are in small business. Small companies offer greater flexibility and the prospect of real responsibility earlier on in their career. Next time you see a big firm's glossy recruitment brochure, ask yourself, 'if these firms are really so brilliant and do offer a life beyond compare, why do they have to work so hard to convince people to join?'3

Back to the young ones...

You are now probably wondering how and where to begin. The first step to landing your dream job is choosing the right degree. Read Chapter 2 to find out how.

---

3 *The Pinstriped Prison*, p.61

Chapter 2: Choosing a degree— "happiness leads to success"

Choosing the degree that is right for YOU (not your parents!)

High school is almost over, just a few more months until you graduate. For many of you, university is next on the list—your brilliant and successful career is getting closer.

However, this chapter is not just for school leavers— unfortunately, many young people have chosen the wrong degree. Some of you may have even finished that degree. So, if you are going to keep studying, this chapter is also for you.

Moving into the next phase of your education can be daunting and a bit terrifying. Suddenly there are big decisions to make, such as:

Which university to go to?
What course to study?
Is university the only option?

It can get really confusing and hard to avoid feeling overwhelmed by it all. When it comes to deciding your future, it's important to take the time to think about it, to consider every angle, and to make sure you're making the right decision for you.

The best kept secret...

Too many people think they go to uni to learn how to balance books or how to use statistics. What they fail to understand is that uni is really about learning how to think and how to research

7 Not so-good reasons for choosing a degree

1. I've got the marks, why waste them?

2. Mum (or Dad) did it, so I should too

3. My mates are all doing it

4. People will be impressed if I study Arts, Law, or Medicine

5. People in that industry make a lot of money

6. I can get into uni, bad marks and all—see sidenote ***

7. Maybe I'll study Business over English because it has a better reputation

*** A sidenote from the 'Grey Guru'

"'My marks were so low that I was lucky to have been accepted into university at all', said one of my daughter's friends when she enrolled.

After six weeks, she had dropped out and now has a nice $2,700 HECS debt to pay off. An extreme case, but all too common.

If you are the sort of person who wants to get cracking on a career now, then get a job and start a certificate or diploma. You'll have more **choices** after a couple of years working. Plus, you will be more likely to know the best degree to help you get that dream job."

When It Comes To Parents...

We hate to say it, but it's a good idea to ignore your parents when deciding what degree to undertake. They want the best for you, but sometimes their advice can be detrimental to your time at university, damaging your career in the long run (unintentionally, of course). Ultimately, what they care about is for you to find a good job and enjoy it. However, their ideas about what you should be doing may be completely different to yours and the practical advice in this book. Sometimes, their experience and values get in the way of what's really right for you, pushing you in the wrong direction (like studying Medicine when you would really love to run a small business).

They may not even realise that they're hurting your chances of landing your dream job when they say things like:

"Why do you want to do that? Are you crazy?"

Or

"Oh. No, you can't do that."

Information:

Some high school kids either couldn't be bothered to research into uni degrees, or they're under the misconception that they already know all that they need to, and any additional information would be useless. **Wrong.**

If the way you go about choosing three or four years of hard work is just off a hunch that you might like the course, or you *think* you want to work in that area, don't be surprised when you become bored, restless, and ready to throw in the towel.

Think you want to do a degree in Psychology because you're a great listener? Did you know you'd need even more schooling after you've received your undergraduate degree if you want to practice as a psychologist? That's the sort of thing people who do too little research find out half way through their second year. If you're not prepared to stay at uni a couple of years longer, then all you will have is a degree and not much else.

Don't go into a three-year degree program only to find out—a semester away from graduating—that it's absolutely useless to you. We'll talk about getting all the information you need a bit later on in the chapter.

Here is where you should concentrate...

7 GREAT reasons for choosing a degree

Important pointers for making the right decision:

1. You'll enjoy what you will be studying and learning

2. It'll teach you how to learn and research and apply these methods to your future career, as well as everyday life

3. It leaves you enough time to get that all-important work experience

4. It keeps your options open, as it is a more general degree— see sidenote ***

5. You haven't made a hasty decision and have thought it through

6. You've figured out what you love doing or at least enjoy

7. You've made the decision for yourself, not for your parents, teachers, or career advisor

***A sidenote from the 'Grey Guru'

"General degrees are those that are useful for many different careers. Way too many people do what I call trade degrees, like Accounting or Law, or even the egregious Media Studies. These degrees narrow your options, and are full of facts you may forget and that employers won't value. The classic general degree is, of course, Arts."

Doing what you love:

Some people <u>really</u> underestimate the value of pursuing a degree or a career that they'll actually enjoy doing. Research shows that productivity and efficiency soar when people are doing work that they actually like. Yes, it's true—when you're happy with what you're doing, you'll put more energy and passion into your work.

Too many people choose degrees to impress people, to satisfy their parents' wants, or they just go along with the herd. They're not doing themselves any favours. If you choose your degree <u>just</u> to get a job, life could get a bit boring.

How can you find success or enjoyment if you wake up thinking, "I *really* don't want to go to this lecture, it bores the pants off me". Unsurprisingly, this sort of thinking will carry over to your working life. Don't waste your time, money, or energy on a degree you don't enjoy. Why come out of university with a degree you can't even use?

Still not convinced about this whole 'happiness leads to success' theory?

See if the following story changes your mind.

There was once a student of Reed College in Portland, Oregon. He went to university, mainly to satisfy the wishes of his parents. After six months, he couldn't see the value in university, so he dropped out. He didn't know what he wanted to do in life, and couldn't see how being stuck in a lecture hall was going to help him see the light.

Considering that he didn't have to take any 'required' courses, he started taking classes he was actually interested in. One of these was a calligraphy class. At the same time, he was crashing at friends' places and struggling to make ends meet. In his classes, he learned all about different typefaces—from spacing, to combinations. For him it was fascinating and he couldn't have been happier.

Ten years later, this man became a part of the team that founded Apple and started developing Macintosh computers. Steve Jobs, a young college dropout, remembered the calligraphy classes he had taken and used it in designing the very first Mac. It was the first computer with 'beautiful' typography. Windows followed suit and suddenly every computer had hundreds of different fonts.

Today, he's worth billions and those of us who have iPhones truly appreciate his genius.

Find what you love and what you enjoy. Follow your passion and you will be happy. You're far more likely to succeed by taking this approach.

What to consider when making your decision:

You need to decide what the best possible degree is for <u>you</u>. Your first step should be to take a long, hard look at yourself. The more you understand yourself (your **wants** and **needs)**, the easier it will be to determine what you want in a degree. So here are some things that may help you in deciding.

Your interests:

If you aren't going to study something that interests you, it's going to be a very long three, four, or even five years. You'll just be wasting your time and money. Success will come if you enjoy what you're doing. Think about any class or activity that you've enjoyed and what it was that you liked about them?

Your talents:

What are you good at? Maybe you have a flair for writing or a knack for numbers. Identify your skills and abilities, and have a look to see what degrees could suit your strong points. Be sure that the sorts of things you'll learn will be valued or useful in your future career—see sidenote ***.

*** A sidenote from the 'Grey Guru'

"My son Guy is just finishing an Arts degree, & he (and his parents) copped all the usual questions:

"What will you do when you finish (with a concerned, sceptical look on their faces)?"

Or...

"What sort of career will that be useful for (with a condescending look)?"

Guy chose courses that he found interesting and challenging. He also applied for an unpaid internship at one of Australia's most creative and dynamic advertising agencies, and was very pleased when he landed it— they get 10 applicants a week.

So, what were the subject choices that the advertising agency really valued?

Sociology and English

Guy worked unpaid for 3 days a week for 7 months. Finally, they offered him a full-time job as a Strategic Planner. Not bad for a 22 year-old, but he had definitely paid his dues to get there. "

Your career prospects:

Have no clue what you'd like to do when you're all grown up? Don't worry, many people don't and they spend most of their uni careers transferring from one degree to another. Trust us, this is a long, laborious, and frustrating experience. While it's a good idea to consider what you'd like to do after uni, your decision **should not** solely be based on this. Having an idea of what you *may* want to do will help point you in the right direction of your uni degree choice. Instead of thinking, "well, everyone should have a good knowledge about business", and picking a Business Administration degree, choose a more general degree. Something like a Bachelor of Arts gives you the freedom to basically do any subject and explore your options.

7 Questions to ask yourself—get a better understanding of you:

1. Do you enjoy hands-on work?

2. Do you work well with people?

3. How do you handle pressure?

4. Are you confident?

5. Do you prefer to be behind the scenes?

6. Do you like to help people?

7. Do you like to travel?

> By answering some of these questions, you could be one step closer to identifying the degree that best suits you.

How to get the information you need:

It's not enough to just say "well, I enjoy numbers so I'm going to study Accounting". You still need to do your research to see if this is the right degree for you. There are a number of places where you can get the information that will help you.

University handbooks:

These will be able to tell you all about the different degree programs that are offered and all that they entail. You'll be able to see all the subjects you'll need to take, how long the degree should take you, and even possible career prospects. Make a list of your options and eliminate the degrees that don't interest you.

Lecturers or the Heads of Departments:

If a degree seems appealing, make an appointment with a lecturer and ask them all the questions you have about the course. Have some questions ready so you're not wasting their time trying to think of them on the spot.

Some questions you can ask:

- What does the course involve?

- What are the assessments like? What are some examples?

- How many hours of study and homework should do in to be successful?

- What careers follow from this degree?

- How useful is this degree in finding a job in _____?

- How easy is it for new graduates to land work with this degree?

- What proportion of graduates went into which jobs in the last few years?

Other students:

Find students in their second or third year and ask them about the degree—what they like, what they don't like, what it involves, how many hours a week are dedicated to study, etc. If you don't know anybody to contact, try waiting outside a lecture hall or ask your friends if they know someone. Don't just rely on one person's opinion—get a few as everyone has had different experiences.

People who work in the field that you are considering:

Try to find two or three people and ask them how they got to where they are now. Ask them what degree they have and how it helped them (they could be one of the many who got a degree completely irrelevant to their job, or no degree at all!). You'll also be able to get an insight into the job itself. By asking exactly what it involves, you may find it's the wrong career prospect for you. You will never find that out unless you go out and get the information.

Work experience:

Internships, volunteer work, or part-time employment <u>will</u> help you explore your career options and decide if that job is the right choice for you. They will give you the opportunity to develop your skills in the areas that interest you, as well as your transferable skills. Work experience is also a great way to start networking and get in touch with contacts that may be useful later on (see Ch. 4).

Known as 'America's greatest marketer', and the author of the New York Times Best Seller, "Permission Marketing: Turning Strangers Into Friends and Friends Into Customers", **Seth Godin** has something to say about the power of gaining work experience.

When two Harvard Business School students asked for his advice on how to find marketing jobs, Seth's response was, "Go to a small company, work for the CEO, get a job where you actually get to make mistakes and do something".

Like Seth, we know that experience is an important asset that employers find highly valuable.

Seth also places a large emphasis on the freedom of choice and that <u>happiness leads to success</u> when it comes to choosing a degree:

> *"The best part of college is that you could become whatever you wanted to become, but most people just do what they think they must. It was a tremendous gift—the ability to choose."*

The first step is always the hardest...

Now you know the how to go about choosing a degree that is tailored to your needs. Read Chapter 3 to learn about the job-hunting strategies that will help you land your ideal career.

Chapter 3: Job Hunting Strategies

The First Steps to Getting That DREAM Job

We know you're still young and you think you've got years to go until you have to consider your future— you're wrong. There's no time like the present to start thinking about what you'll need to do to get that dream job.

Think of yourself as a product...

If you really want a chance at landing your ideal career, you need to understand that you have to sell yourself. No one else is going to do it for you, so off your butt and start selling!

We're going to go ahead and assume none of you are salespeople, but just try and imagine what it would be like to pitch a product to a customer—a product that you really don't know all that much about. You can explain what it looks like, but that's about it. You have no idea of its functions or capabilities. What chance do you think you have of getting that sale? **Zero.**

If you thought any more than that, you're sadly mistaken. In order to sell yourself to employers, you need to understand yourself. What are your passions? What are your goals? It's extremely important to plan ahead and to be focused on your future. It will make it easier to get to where you want to be.

7 Ways you will get to where you want to be

1. Having the qualifications

2. Having a plan of action

3. Enthusiasm for your job or career

4. Having mentors to help guide and support you

5. Having work experience

6. Taking action for the things you need to do

7. Accepting that some things happen with time

Turning Your Career Dreams Into a Reality...

Here's some good news: You don't have to have a 60-page document that details your career plan. It only needs to be one page.

To make your plan, you need to:

- Work out what you want to do

- Who you want to do it with

- Go and see them and talk about how you can help them and make them money

One-Page Plans should:

Be simple

Be short and straight forward

Easily revisable

WHERE

1. _____
2. _____

WHAT

1. _____ 2. _____
3. _____ 4. _____
5. _____ 6. _____
7. _____ 8. _____

WHICH

1. _____ 2. _____
3. _____ 4. _____
5. _____ 6. _____
7. _____ 8. _____

VALUES

1. _____
2. _____
3. _____

ACTION

NOW   NEXT 3 MONTHS

1. _____ 1. _____
2. _____ 2. _____

NETWORK TARGETS

INDUSTRY ASSOCIATIONS   PEOPLE

1. _____ 1. _____
2. _____ 2. _____

WHERE do you want to work?

Many people don't even think about this and it's usually the simplest thing to work out. If you're completely flexible where you're willing to work, then it might be a lot easier to write down where you *don't* want to work.

Start by asking these questions...

- Is there a particular country you'd like to live and work in?
- What sort of climate would you like to work in?
- What kind of lifestyle are you looking for?
- Is work available for you in that area?

Of course, the reality for many young graduates with loans to pay off is that they need to live at home for a while.

WHAT do you want to do?

What aspects of a job, any job in the world, would make you jump out of bed in the morning? List, and then rank them.

> What talents or skills can you offer?
> What field would you like to work in?
> What are your interests?

It's a good idea to actually speak to people in the industry you'd like to work in. Sometimes, we put jobs up on a pedestal without knowing much about them. If you ask someone the positive and negative aspects of a job, it might give you a more accurate picture of that particular career path.

WHICH company do you want to work for?

Obviously, you can only answer this question when you know what kind of industry you'd like to work in. Once you know this, research different businesses in that industry and make a short list. Your research may lead you to change your preferences or even cross off an organisation you thought you'd be great for—see sidenote ***.

***A sidenote from the 'Grey Guru'

"'The road less travelled' is often, if not always, the best road. It's simple advice, but look where everyone else is applying and go elsewhere. In particular, think about smaller companies that most graduates ignore."

Some questions to think about...

- Would you prefer to work for the industry leader or for an organisation in the early growth stage?

- Do you want to be part of a large group, or be more visible in a small organisation?

- Which companies have the ethics, attitudes and values that are most like yours?

- Which companies have the product or service you would be most proud to represent?

- Which are the companies that can provide you with the most opportunities and career growth?

What are your VALUES?

Why do you want to work? Is it that you want to help people? Perhaps you want to make a difference in some way? Or, is financial success a key motivation for you? By discovering what your values are, it might make it easier to pinpoint the right career for you.

Make a list...

Take a look at the following values. See which apply most to you:

Being challenged

Balance between work and social life

Integrity in business dealings

Stable and secure work

Using your creativity

Freedom and flexibility

Having pride in your work

Strong financial rewards

Professional growth and development

Good working relationships

Respect, recognition and being valued

Having autonomy and independence

Novelty and a fast-paced business environment

These are just a few of the hundreds of values you could choose from. Make your list, and narrow it down to 4 core values.

Taking action:

Think about the actions you need to take now and in the next three months. What can you do to get closer to your goal? Landing a great job is about small steps—small actions that work together, until it just seems easy.

Networking:

When developing your career, you can't just rely on the 20% of jobs that are advertised. You need to get out there and network because that's the only way you're going to tap into the hidden job market. Think of the people and groups in the industry you'd like to work in and start building your network.

Networking is CRITICAL to building a dream career, so check out Chapter 4 to find out more.

Chapter 4: Networking

The importance of networking: It is time to access that hidden job market!

Did you know that only 10 – 20 % of job openings are ever publicly known?

So, if you aren't making your way into the hidden job market, you're closing yourself off from 80% of the jobs that are on offer.

It doesn't have to be this way and this is where networking comes in. For those of you who aren't quite sure what networking is, it basically involves building relationships and using these connections to improve your skills and career.

Why is networking so important?

By building a network, you're not only exposing yourself to people whose perspectives, experiences, and knowledge can assist you in deciding your future, but you're also increasing your chances of landing your ideal career. You're giving yourself the opportunity to get great advice from those in the industry.

Many students aren't aware of the importance of networks and creating strong social ties. They're usually happy emailing out their resumes to employers and hoping for the best. A lot of the time, jobs aren't available and when they are, employers have long forgotten where they filed your resume.

Young people also forget that many people come out of university with the same qualifications, and it's the ones who have already made their connections during university who will be landing the dream careers.

Ways That Networking Can Work Wonders For Your Career:

Referrals
Potential employers are way more likely to hire someone who comes recommended by one of their employees or a colleague they trust

Advice
Ask people already working in the field you'd like to work how they got to where they are, and how you could succeed there

Insider information
Be the first to know if there's a job available

Social support
Being a part of a group that can offer advice and assistance is very helpful when trying to shape your career

Better connections increase your job opportunities, your salary, and your overall sense of well-being and belonging.

Not every contact will offer you a job and it may even take a while for them to start giving you any information about job openings. Don't let this get you down because it's important to remember that networking is an ongoing process and is all about building relationships. It's not about going to one cocktail party or industry sponsored breakfast and walking out with your ideal job in hand.

The early bird gets the worm...

Don't wait until you've graduated from university—start networking early. Your lecturers, tutors, and even your fellow students have connections that could be of use to you. They'll be able to give you invaluable advice, feedback, and support.

Not really sure how to foster these relationships? Sign up for department clubs and organisations, or speak to lecturers and tutors out of class time. Departmental events and conferences are also a great way to meet some useful contacts. Don't become another one of the 90% of students who don't know how to network. Be in the 10% minority of networkers—it will give you a huge advantage.

"I already have heaps of friends and family who know some people."

Sadly, this just isn't going to cut it. We're not dismissing the power of friends and families—sometimes they are truly helpful. However, it's the people furthest from you who are going to be the most helpful. We all assume our friends and family know us best. Unfortunately, that's wrong; we only think they do. They don't know what we *really* want from our careers.

The 'Theory of Weak Ties' tells us that the benefits from social networks are much higher when ties among people in the network are weak. They let you get away from your narrow social circle, letting you explore your options and different environments. This theory stresses that weak ties are far more effective for 'well-educated job-seekers'.

Here's another fun fact about weak ties: higher wages, more job satisfaction, and a closer relationship between job and university degrees are more likely to be associated with weak ties being used in finding employment.

Maximise your opportunities by getting out there, going to seminars, and functions. Go and talk to a few complete strangers—you might surprise yourself by making a new connection, dramatically improving your chances of landing a dream job later on. What have you got to lose?

7 Tips for making strong connections

1. Don't stand in the corner and watch *others* meet new people

2. It's not about pampering people with compliments; it's about networking

3. Meet people in person— telephone calls and emails come later on

4. Stay focused on the person you're talking to

5. Prepare two or three questions you can comfortably ask strangers—see sidenote***

6. You're not there to chat about the latest Hollywood gossip— let them know your strengths and career goals

7. Just like any other relationship, building networks takes time

---

*** A sidenote from the 'Grey Guru'

"When networking at a function or event, it is crucial to ask appropriate questions that not only help you to gain information, but that you can also ask a stranger comfortably. Try using an ice-breaker question:

What is the main benefit you've gained from being a member of [this group]?

What was the highlight of your day? Weekend? Last week?

How long have you been coming to these functions?

Don't focus on negative topics. Try to keep it light and interesting and always stay fully focused with the person you are talking to. Giving someone 60 seconds of uninterrupted time and eye contact is always better than ten minutes of only half paying attention, with your eyes darting around the room."

How to build your network:

It's all well and good that you *know* networking is going to be beneficial to your career, but now you have to get out there and actually start making contact with people who could help you push your career forward.

Networking hotspots you need to know about:

Functions, seminars & conferences:

You're there to make a good impression, so it's really important to look and act professional. Like we said, sitting in a corner isn't going to get you anywhere. Mingle, go and introduce yourself to people—new people who you've never met before. Don't talk about your favourite TV shows or your thoughts on global warming. Let people know your careers aspirations, like what you're studying, and where you see yourself in five years time. Be sure to keep the personal chat and facts about yourself to a minimum. Focus on the other person and see if you can find ways to help them—see sidenote***.

*** A sidenote from the 'Grey Guru'

"When talking about how to act and look professional at a function or event, it is also important to know how to appropriately 'escape'.

Your goal is to leave the conversation graciously and allow for an easy start to a new conversation when you next meet. Do this by:

Trying to look for a future activity to share.

Creating future opportunities together.

If you have promised something, repeat it e.g. "I'll be sending you _____."

Sometimes it is necessary to escape.

Ways to do this might be to perhaps introduce someone else or ask for their card before politely excusing yourself.

Don't say what so many self-important people do: 'I'll be back in a second', and you don't see them again. Such behaviour recalls the popular saying: 'be nice to those you pass on your way up, as you'll get to know them again on the way down'.

7 Things to do & *not* do at a function

1. **Do** give people a reason to want you in their network. Help them in any way you can, without expecting any rewards
2. **Don't** go there without some business cards. They don't have to be fancy or glossy, they just need to let people know how to get in contact with you
3. **Do** ask for their business card. Write the event and date on the back of the card. Keep an Excel spreadsheet that records, who, when, and where you met someone
4. **Don't** let fear and shyness get to you—start introducing yourself
5. **Do** let people know what you're good at, your goals and interests. Keep it short, then focus on them
6. **Do** arrive early and leave late. There are no speeches keeping you glued to your seat so you're free to meet people and make connections before and after the formal bits—see sidenote***
7. **Do** follow up with a short email letting them know it was nice to meet them

***A sidenote from the *'Grey Guru'*

Be sure to 'work' a conference, before and after the formal bits. Arrive early or leave late or better still, do both. If the invitation says 5 for 5:30 pm, then 5.05pm is a great time to arrive. The effective connecting happens before and after the function, when there is no official programme keeping you locked to your chair (or quietly listening to speeches). Staying after the official program ends is also a great time to network, and at this point you also have the benefit of the seminar content to talk about. This makes for easy conversation opening.

Lots of busy people arrive late and leave early, missing the opportunities that are available. It's far better to go to fewer functions and get value out of them. If possible, ask for a list of attendees before the event. Then you can target the people you really want or need to make contact with."

Somewhere a bit more informal:

We mentioned your lecturers and classmates, but try meeting some new people at social or sporting events. Join a university soccer team, or a department trivia club. You never know who will be a part of these teams, or who they may know. Let your fingers do the walking:

Find contacts using the Internet or industry guides. These could all be potential employers, or a means of finding your ideal career.

Hint: Research the contact before you call them. Prepare what you want to say.

Information interviews:

Not everyone thinks you're a nuisance or being pushy when you ask for help and advice. Email a few people in the industry you'd like to work in and ask for a few minutes of their time. Make sure they know you're not coming in to ask for a job, just for some of their wisdom and knowledge. If your intention was to go in and ask for a job, don't expect much. Your contact may say, "I'll see what I can do", which usually leads to zero job offers.

Ask them questions like:

How did you get your first job in ____?

How well did university (or your degree) prepare you for this job?

I'm interested in learning more about ____

What did you learn from your first job?

What advice can you give me to advance my career?

Networking online:

Almost all of you use Facebook and/or other social networking sites. Yes, we know, social networking is a great way to keep in contact with friends, and upload new photos from the previous weekend. But it is also useful in making connections that can help your career.

Ways To Use Online Networking To Your Advantage:

Be careful with your online profile. It's not uncommon for employers to do some research about you before an interview so be careful with what you put online. No embarrassing pictures from a crazy party, no foul language—nothing that can harm your reputation. Remember, once it's out there, there's always a way to find it. If you do feel the need to have an outrageous profile, put it under a pseudonym and have a second profile under your real name. Be overt with information regarding your career, interests, and goals.

Further, try to be selective of who's in your network. It's important that they actually know who you are, have a good opinion of you and would recommend you.

7 Tips for Successful Networking

If you forget all the other advice, at least remember these
key points

1. Helping others comes first—see sidenote ***

2. Show an interest in others. Don't do all the talking, and be sure
to ask them relevant questions about their job, or the training
they endured to get to where they are. Listen to their answers

3. You need to be proactive. Get outside of your comfort zone
and talk to people

4. Follow up on any advice you are given

5. When in an information interview or in casual conversation,
have an equal balance between asking questions, sharing
something about yourself, and listening to others' responses

6. Communication is key. When you're telling people about
yourself, what and how you say it is important in their decision to
help you out or not

7. Whether they refer you to someone or not, thank them.
Networking is all about building and maintaining relationships

*** A sidenote from the 'Grey Guru'

"Just because you're a uni student doesn't
mean that there aren't ways for you to assist
those oh-so important businessmen and women.
Here are some ways you can help them:

Share research

Help them with new technology. One of the advantages of being a product of Generation Y is that you are miles ahead in that department. Perhaps they need advice on fixing a computer, or maybe they want to buy a new plasma TV, and don't know which is the best kind

Help them understand the youth market place

Tap them into part-time workers and let them know if you have friends who are looking for work

Inform them about the benefits of hiring good graduates. You could help save them hours of useless interviews"

Time to get started...

It is now time to start applying for your dream job, and this process begins with an outstanding cover letter. Read Chapter 5 to learn how to 'wow' employers with your cover letter, and why they are so important.

Chapter 5: The Awful Truth About Recruitment Firms

What to know and look out for when dealing with recruitment agencies.

You've tried the job search on your own, Seek.com.au has become your homepage, you never leave the classifieds section of the paper unread, and still, you're jobless. Another avenue people choose to explore is a recruitment agency. It's their job to help you land your ideal job and they'll stop at nothing until you're earning a steady income.

The sad truth...

If this is your thought process, it may come as a shock to find out that there is an overwhelming dislike of recruiters and recruitment companies amongst current job seekers. They're just not as helpful as you'd like them to be. Put simply, they have their own agendas—they are trying to make a living just like everyone else. When you know that they are paid on commission by companies to find them staff, it's pretty obvious where their loyalties lie.

Many job seekers find that their calls are not returned, they rarely receive any feedback and are often pushed back to square one: job-less.

Shocking Statistics:

- 95% of people who dealt with recruitment firms never had their calls returned

- Over 90% had been ignored more than once

- More than 50% had been ignored many times

A sidenote from the 'Grey Guru'

"I worked in the recruitment industry for 20 years, and during that time I formed a pretty low opinion of it. In a nutshell, most recruiters are self-serving salesmen with appalling ethics. As a young person entering the workforce, be wary of them!"

A lot of the time, applicants feel like *they're* to blame and it's their own fault for not having the skills and experience to get the job (or even a response). No one ever looks to place blame with the recruiters who are 'too busy' or too rude to return a call.

After several unanswered phone calls, you're bound to feel irritated. So feel free to let them know that you won't take their rudeness sitting down. Send them what we like to call the **'Unhappy Applicant Email'**. If you *really* want them to know how unhappy you are, send a copy to their Managing Director.

Unhappy Applicant Email:

To: BobSmith@megarecruit.com.au
CC: MarytheCEO@megarecruit.com.au
Subject: Job number X437

Dear Bob,

I have made a number of calls to your office and would appreciate some feedback.

To save time for both of us, perhaps just cut and paste
one of the following into the subject line and
 hit Reply:

- I'm sorry, I've been ill, and will call you shortly
- You've got the job but I've forgotten to let you know
- You're 'on hold' in case the leading applicant falls over
- I no longer recruit for that employer
- Bob no longer works for the firm (PA please complete)
- You are not on the short list and are unlikely to be
- I have lost your resume and would like a new copy

I look forward to your response.

Yours sincerely,

Tom Winters

They are not as useful as you think...

Most people use recruitment firms because they like to think that they are these all-knowing beings who have access to hundreds upon hundreds of jobs. If a job exists, recruitment firms know about it.

Like so many other assumptions—wrong

Let's do some maths...

80% of jobs are never advertised, they're part of the hidden job market

Of the other **20%**, that are, half are advertised by the company itself

This means recruiters only have access to about **10%** of the job market. Remember, there isn't just one recruitment firm out there, so this 10% is further reduced

At the very most, a big recruitment firm may only have access to **5%** of these jobs

Less than one in twenty jobs are available through a particular recruiter

Not quite hundreds upon hundreds of jobs. More like one in one hundred

All is not lost...

Recruiters aren't necessarily all bad; they can be a great source of information. If you can find two or three who you can form a good relationship with (see Chapter 4), you're a couple of steps closer to landing the perfect job.

The value exchange

- Building networks is all about giving and receiving

- If you <u>give</u> recruiters referrals to candidates or potential clients, you may <u>receive</u> information on other positions that they know about

Remember, respecting confidentiality and privacy is really important, so don't share information that you shouldn't.

"How do I find someone to help me?"

A useful way to find a recruiter is to go through old job advertisements online and in the newspaper. If you do this three or four times, leaving a month in between, you'll be able to find a recruitment agency that regularly advertises jobs in the field you'd like to work in. Make a list of a few names, call them up, and tell them why you'd like to meet with them.

Another way to network with recruiters is to choose one you've met through your job search.

Note: You'd be better off choosing one you got along with!

7 Things to keep in mind when dealing with

recruiters

1. They're the gatekeepers to jobs, so help them to help you

2. You may need to remind them who you are. Their databases aren't too reliable

3. Always look for feedback – it'll help you for next time

4. If you don't expect anything from them, you'll be pleasantly surprised

5. Do expect them to sell hard when it comes to the job offer

6. They are not career experts

7. If you've been interviewed and had none of your phone calls returned, send them that Unhappy Applicant email

Time to get started....

It is now time to start applying for your dream job, and this process begins with an outstanding cover letter. Read Chapter 6 to learn how to 'wow' employers with your cover letter, and why they are so important.

Chapter 6: Cover Letters

The truth about cover letters—we hate to break it to you, but sometimes you can really judge a book by its cover!

Your cover letter is the first impression you give an employer, so make sure you leave them wanting more.

"Why bother? Shouldn't my resume be enough?"

Put simply—no.

Your cover letter is your sales pitch; it's your door opener. Without a great cover letter, many employers won't even read the resume you've spent hours working on.

Sad, but true

You need a cover letter so that...

Your resume ends up in **the right hands**—you don't want it tossed aside with the rubbish, do you?

You have a chance to **SELL, SELL, SELL!** This is your opportunity to boast about all of your skills. Think of your cover letter as your bait to reel the employer in.

Let's face it; employers and recruiters are busy people. They have many resumes and cover letters to sift through each day and don't have the time to go looking into the deeper meaning behind your words. So, don't ramble, just get straight to the point.

7 Handy hints for a great cover letter:

1. Keep it short and straight forward
2. Use three or four paragraphs maximum
3. Have three key points you want the employer to read when they open your letter. Make sure these key points are tailored to the job
4. Let them know what you can offer them
5. Utilise the same key words used in the job advertisement. Be careful not to use too many or you'll risk looking like you are trying too hard
6. Proofread, edit and polish. Make sure that there are no spelling or grammatical errors
7. We'll leave this one for later in the chapter. It's worth the wait!

Things that need to be in your cover letter:

It doesn't matter what kind of cover letter you're sending (don't worry, we'll get to the different types of cover letters shortly), there are a few essential, *non-negotiable,* things that need to be included.

Your address:

This should go in the top left-hand corner of the letter. There is no need to put your name, telephone number, or date of birth. These all go on your resume.

The name of the employer:

Address the letter to the person who will be reading it, followed by the company name. There's no need to put the address of the company on the letter, they know where they are located.

So, why is it important to address your letter to a specific person? Think about it this way: you receive a letter in the mail and it says, "Dear person." Would you read it? *No.*

So what if the advertisement doesn't tell you who you need to address your cover letter to? Well, find out! Call, email, Google search—do anything and everything you can to find out who may be your future employer. Chances are that your competitors haven't even thought about this, so by addressing your cover letter to the person who will be reading your resume, you're already one <u>big</u> step ahead.

Hint: When you address your cover letter to a specific person, end it with, 'Yours Sincerely'. We know, its old-fashioned, but it is also courteous and adds edge to your cover letter.

The reference number:

Most of the time, a job advertisement will have a reference number that you'll need to quote when applying. This helps employers to recognise exactly what job you're applying for. The less confused they are, the more chances you have of getting an interview.

The start:

You can set yourself apart from the rest by *not* starting with:

'I wish to apply for the job advertised on...'

Or

'I saw the job for ... advertised and I would like to apply'

Try starting with a sentence that shows how enthusiastic you are for this particular job role. Why not try something like:

'I am very interested in the role of...'

Or

"I am eager to learn more about the position that was advertised in the...."

First paragraph:

This is where you catch the employer's attention. You need to make a powerful and lasting impression. Focus on two or three points that you *want*, and *need* to be read. Be sure to make these relevant to the specific job you are applying for.

Second paragraph:

Show them you've really paid attention to what they've asked for in the advertisement. Match your skills and qualities to what they're looking for. Use phrases like, *'In addition, I am...'* or *'Furthermore, I have demonstrated this skill...'* to draw attention to something unique or special about yourself.

Reread the advertisement to ensure you have all the facts you need so that you know exactly what your potential employer expects of an employee. So, they need someone with enthusiasm and drive? What a coincidence! Those are the exact qualities you have. Just to be clear, you actually *should* have these qualities. If you don't, maybe you should be applying for something else because lying gets you nowhere fast. The second paragraph is all about making it simple for the employer to see that you are the perfect candidate for the position.

The strong finish:

Employers don't have the patience for all those wishy-washy sign-offs. Don't use any of the following as you will be stating the obvious:

- *'Please find my resume attached to the email.'* <u>Of course</u> you've attached your resume! You wouldn't get very far if you hadn't

- *'I am available for an interview.'* If you weren't available, you shouldn't have applied for the position

- *'If you have any questions, please don't hesitate to call me.'* You've already provided your contact details in your resume, and they'll decide to call you or not, regardless of your invitation

This finishing paragraph needs to show enthusiasm, optimism, and most importantly assertiveness. Statements like, "I am confident that I have the skills, qualities and knowledge appropriate for this particular position," show them you've got confidence in yourself and are the right person for the job.

So, are you ready for it? The 7th handy hint that'll guarantee your cover letter won't get tossed?

7 Take control of the process

Don't wait for them to get back to you. All that will happen is that you'll sit around, twiddling your thumbs, worrying where your cover letter and resume have ended up. As Gran says, "worrying is like a rocking chair; it gives you something to do, but it doesn't get you anywhere". What does this mean? Worrying is a waste of time. So this is how you should conclude your letter:

'I will contact you next week to discuss the suitability of my application.'

This gets their attention and gives them something to prepare for. Whether they're going to reject you or not, your name and your impending call will be in the back of their minds. They're thinking about *you!*

Time To Get Specific...

Now that you've read through all the 'general rules' of the cover letter, it's important to understand that there are different types of cover letters. They're more or less the same, but you just need to be aware of different ways to tweak them. A cover letter that responds to an advertisement will sound a little different to one that is sent in hopes of an unadvertised position being available.

Cover letter 1: "I am eager to apply for..."

This cover letter is used when you're responding to an advertisement. Using the advice we gave you earlier in the chapter, here is an example:

Address: 12 Principal St,

Rockdale

NSW 2216

Email: tomwinters@gmail.com

H: (02) 91 234 567

M: 0412 345 678

Mr. Smith,

The Job Factory

27 April 2009

Ref no 99876

Dear Mr. Smith,

I was very interested when I came across the job advertised in the Rockdale Post for the position of Part-Time Customer Service Supervisor in the Job Factory. I believe that I have the attributes and experience to excel in this position. In my current position, I employ an array of communication skills while serving customers and working within a team environment. I also have strong organisational skills and have had experience with banking duties.

I can offer a happy disposition, commitment, and have the ability to work well both unsupervised and as part of a team. I am a hard worker and can cope well under pressure I believe that my experience working at Flexible Development Solutions has trained and prepared me for any challenges that may arise.

I am excited about the possibility of working with The Job Factory. I will contact you within the next week to discuss the suitability of my application.

Yours sincerely,

Tom Winters

Hint: Make sure you've read the advertisement carefully because there are always little clues as to what the employer is looking for.

When they say:

'Bright, motivated, self-starter'

They mean:

Happy, clever, doesn't need much help to get going

When they say:

'Can look forward to the challenge of working in a fast-moving environment'

They mean:

Able to deal with problems and handle pressure

By understanding what they mean, you'll more easily be able to tailor your letter *exactly* to their needs.

Cover letter 2: "I am looking for..."

You saw an advertisement for your dream job that was published a couple of months earlier. You didn't apply and you think you've missed your chance. However, you could always send through a speculative cover letter and resume. What this style of cover letter and resume sets out to do is inquire about a previously advertised position, and show your attributes and qualities that fit the mould for this position.

If you don't remember the name of the contact person, do your research and find out. Is there a company that you really want to work for but you've never seen them advertise positions? Who cares! Try your luck because you never know what they'll say. They may be so impressed with your initiative that they'll find something for you to do, even if it is getting coffee and making photocopies. A foot in the door is the opportunity you need to climb and reach your dream career—see sidenote ***.

***A sidenote from the 'Grey Guru'

"A foot in the door is <u>way</u> more than a foot in the door, if it is the <u>right</u> door for you.

In my talks to graduating classes at universities, I have told students that how you choose where to work when you graduate should be decided on:

Most importantly, is it the **right company** for you? See if they meet the criteria on your One-Page plan

Is the person you'll be working for someone you **respect**, who will **mentor** and **support** you?

What will you actually be doing in the first 6 months?

Note: A good company will have you doing something better so fast it will give you no regrets for making coffee for the first month.

I read 7 books on career advice when researching for my 2 books, including 2 written specifically for young people. Why do none of these books make this point? They were written by *psychologists*.

They've never worked in a job where they manage people, make things, or deliver a service. They can't see the bigger picture.

Also, an even <u>less</u> important reason for taking your first professional job is for the money. Good companies and good bosses will pay you what you're worth pretty quickly."

The speculative cover letter is almost exactly the same as the letter we showed you before, just with a few minor changes.

Address: 12 Principal St,

Rockdale

NSW 2216

Email: tomwinters@gmail.com

H: (02) 91 234 567

M: 0412 345 678

Mr. Smith

The Job Factory

27 April 2009

Dear Mr. Smith,

I am interested in applying for any possible vacancies your company may have within the customer service department. I have the skills and experience to excel within your company. My current position involves using an array of communication skills while serving customers and working in a team environment. I also have strong organisational skills and have had experience with banking duties.

I can offer a happy disposition, commitment, and have the ability to work well both unsupervised and as part of a team. I am a hard worker and can cope well under pressure. I believe that my two years of experience working at Flexible Development Solutions has trained and prepared me to handle any challenges that may arise.

I have always wanted to work in a customer service role and would love a chance to meet with you. I will contact you within the next week to discuss the potential of a role within The Job Factory.

Yours sincerely,

Tom Winters

Cover letter 3: "I heard it on the grapevine..."

You don't need to spend countless hours scanning Seek or the MyCareer section of the newspaper to find your dream job. Sometimes, Aunt Suzy's, best friend's, husband's nephew knows someone who works in the Human Resources department of the company you'd like to work for, and guess what? They're looking for a graduate just like you! There's no shame in applying for a job just because you've heard about it on the grapevine. And when you do, you need to have a cover letter that suits this situation.

Address: 12 Principal St,

Rockdale

NSW 2216

Email: tomwinters@gmail.com

H: (02) 91 234 567

M: 0412 345 678

Mr. Smith

The Job Factory

27 April 2009

Re: Customer Service Role

Dear Mr. Smith,

I understand from your employee, Mr James Helpful, that The Job Factory has an opening for a part-time customer service supervisor. Mr Helpful has explained the role and duties involved to me and I would like to apply for the position if it is still available, as I have the skills and experience to excel. With my current employer, I use an array of communication skills while serving customers and working within a team environment. I also have strong organisational skills and have had experience with banking duties.

I can offer a happy disposition, commitment, and have the ability to work well both unsupervised and as part of a team. I am a hard worker and can cope well under pressure, and also believe that my two years of experience working at Flexible Development Solutions have trained and prepared me to handle any challenges that may arise.

The Job Factory has always appealed to me as an employer as the staff-customer relationship is well known as one of the best in the industry.

I have always wanted to work in a customer service role and would love a chance to meet with you. I will contact you next week to discuss the potential of a role within The Job Factory.

Yours sincerely,

Tom Winters

Hint: It never hurts to show a potential employer that you know a little something about them.

Another thing to note...

Email, rather than post, your cover letter and resume to the business you are applying for. When emailing through your cover letter and resume, attach them in one document with the letter separate on the first page. This means you don't have to worry about any formatting crises when the email is opened.

However, this doesn't give you the licence to basically send an empty email. Also, you can't write something along the lines of, "Maaaaate! Would love a job, resume attached. Cheers".

Why not try:

Dear Mr. Smith,

> *My cover letter and resume are in the attached document. Thank you for taking the time to consider my application.*

Yours sincerely,

Tom Winters

Simple.

So, did we miss anything?

If you've already forgotten, here are the 7 *'if you learn nothing else'* tricks that will make your cover letter a winner!

1. Make it short, concise and straight forward
2. **Find out a contact name and use it**
3. Promote yourself! Don't be afraid to gloat a little
4. Customise your letter to the job advertisement. Let them know you are the perfect candidate
5. One page is all you need
6. Proofread and edit your cover letter before you send it to your potential employer
7. Be proactive—don't sit around waiting for that call

You're well and truly on your way...

You now have the knowledge to create the perfect cover letter, and all you need is a winning resume to compliment it. Read Chapter 7 to find out what you have to do to complete the package.

Chapter 7: Resumes

At last! You will get the dream job you desperately want with a resume this amazing!

Discover the most valuable ways of improving your resume and your chances of being the one they hire.

So, you want to apply for a job? You'll need:

A cover letter (see Ch.6)

An amazing resume

Read on to discover how...

I t's happened to all of us—you're thinking about your dream job and you're wondering how on earth you're <u>ever</u> going to get there. Maybe you're even looking at the job advertisement on your computer screen and thinking about applying.

Then comes the fear in the pit of your stomach.

"Why would anyone ever hire me over all the other people who are more qualified, eloquent, experienced, have higher IQs, and are applying for the same job?

There's just no chance, right? Think again.

Do you want to discover what <u>none</u> of the other 'super' applicants knows? Something that's going to be your biggest asset in getting an interview? You're about to get the single most important edge over your competition that will ensure you:

- Don't get weeded out at the very first stage because of simple, stupid mistakes

- Are noticed in a really positive way

- Get the chance to be interviewed

It's a nice thought, isn't it? No waiting around, no calling back countless times to make sure they actually got your resume in the first place. <u>Them</u> calling *you.*

But we're getting ahead of ourselves. You need to uncover the secrets of how to get there first.

7 Crucial things you need to know about a resume:

1. Keep it short: Make sure you are to the point and include the most necessary details that will assist you in getting an interview

2. Spelling and grammar: The perfect resume will be free of any spelling or grammatical mistakes

3. Why not use some bullet points? Use no more than a few short sentences in each section

4. Use reverse chronological order: List your most recent jobs first

5. For each job that you list, it is essential to include your responsibilities and achievements

6. List your referees on a separate page*

7. Always follow up with a phone call

*Note: When listing your **referees** (on a separate page at the very end of your resume), write at the top: "Please do not contact my referees before speaking with me". When and if an employer decides to call one of your referees, they will be prepared and ready to answer all of their questions about you.

Snag that Interview! Avoid "Dear So and So"

As mentioned in Chapter 6, it is vital to pay attention to details like who you are sending your cover letter and resume to. If a cover letter and resume arrives addressed 'To Whom It May Concern' or 'Dear Sir/Madam', then potential employers may toss the application aside. They may already have received anywhere from a dozen to a hundred resumes in just one day, for the same job you're applying for.

We can't stress enough the importance of acknowledging the recipient of your job application. It may be this small detail that sets you apart from other applicants who failed to take the time to perfect their resume.

Remember, your resume is your **advertising campaign** to get you the interviews you want, so target your market properly. If your resume isn't up to scratch, it's likely to end up in the 'No' pile.

Did You Catch That?

Find out the name of the person you're applying to, double check the spelling, and USE IT!

The unpolished, unprofessional resume: "And then I did this & then I did that..."

Your resume needs to present all of the most important information for *this* specific job and fast. You need a clear and concise layout. Do you know how long a resume typically gets looked at before a decision is made about it? Anywhere between twenty seconds and two minutes. Employers are making a decision about your future in that short time. Help them make the right choice for you and do everything you can so that you get that interview. If you want to find out more regarding what <u>not</u> to do when writing a resume, be sure to check out:

http://www.healthalliance.com/college/center/resume/comparison.html

Things that need to be on your resume:

Headings:

Put your name at the top of the page in a font size no bigger than 20 pt. For section headings you don't really want to go bigger than 15 pt. Alternatively, you can leave them the same size as the rest of the text, but be sure to make all headings bold and underlined. These things are really a question of individual style, but typically you want your resume to look professional. Messing around with too many font sizes makes other people's eyes hurt. Use simple labels for the important sections like 'Education' and 'Employment History'.

Objective:

This is a sentence you put close to the top that specifies what your career intentions are. It must be true, but you also need to customise it to suit each different position you're applying for so that it remains relevant.

Note: the objective on your resume at this stage should not be *"to work two to three hours a week from a provided beach house for $85 000 - $100 000 a year,"* even if that's what you're feeling.

Personal Details:

The law says you don't have to put your age on a resume but typically employers want to know. A good list of details to mention about you includes: date of birth, email, mobile and/or home number, and your address. Don't hide your contact details; try to make it easy for employers to get in touch with you. You don't need to include your religion or nationality as they're nobody's business and you're not required to provide this information on your resume—see sidenote ***.

*** A sidenote from the 'Grey Guru'

"It's amazing (and sad) how many times I've heard employers say: "I've never really liked anyone from [name country, often from Asia or the Middle East], they always seem so [name their particular ignorance or prejudice] but Monaz is just so different. Just like an Australian". Set yourself apart from these stereotypes by working hard, and prove that you are the right person for the job."

Education:

This is the section where you include the name of your high school, the year you graduated and university entrance score (your UAI or ATAR if you live in NSW or the ACT, the VCE if you live in VIC) if it was a good mark.

If you're studying at university, you can also add:

- The full-name of the institution e.g. University of New South Wales
- Whether you are a full or part-time student
- Your degree e.g. Bachelor of Finance
- Your expected completion date

Note: Some people include their primary schools in this list, but why waste space?

Casual and part-time work experience:

If you've worked a few casual jobs you can include a description of them here. Use reverse chronological order in this list so that your most recent job is at the top and then work backwards, giving less space to each job as you go. Include approximate date ranges for the amount of time you spent at each job. List your responsibilities and what you learned and achieved from each position. This is **very important**—don't waste an opportunity to put in relevant information, so give details! A person who may hire you would want to know about other times you've been employed; what you did there and what they can expect from you in the future.

If you don't have any experience, do not put this section in your resume. Especially don't put a heading that says 'Work Experience' and put underneath it, 'I don't have work experience', unless you want to give the resume screener a good belly laugh.

Note: If you haven't had any sort of experience, go out and get some—paid or unpaid.

Competency (skills):

Here's where you need to promote yourself. Most people don't know what they're good at or are too modest about it. Ask family and friends (when they're in a good mood) what your strengths are and use some of these. These should be modified to suit the requirements of each job you apply for. The following is a list of strengths you can include if they're relevant:

- Team player
- Excellent attention to detail
- Enthusiastic
- Good leadership skills
- Energetic
- Good communication skills
- Ability to handle pressure
- Ability to take the initiative

You would be mental not to...

When applying for a job, look at the advertisement and try to figure out what the employer is looking for. Make sure your resume shows that you have these skills and abilities.

Qualifications:

Have you completed a TAFE or First Aid course? Put it in there! Make sure you start with the most recent qualification first (unless the most recent is the least important).

Awards:

Leadership and representative positions (school prefect, school or vice-captain, etc.), awards from school/uni or your casual job, or any certificates you've received for volunteering efforts are all great things to have on your resume. As mentioned earlier, don't include information from your time spent at primary school.

Interests:

We strongly recommend that you include <u>a few</u> of your hobbies on your resume. Employers see this as a kind of shorthand way of getting to know you. You should also consider the subtext of your interests; if you put down 'reading' as one your hobbies this suggests you're a solitary kind of person while 'touch football' suggests a team player.

Only list things you're genuinely interested and/or involved in. There's nothing worse than being asked in the interview about a hobby on your resume that you actually know nothing about.

References:

Never put the contact details of your references on your resume. Sometimes, employers will call your references before they even do a phone interview with you as a quick way to screen candidates out. Once you've been short-listed for the job and asked for the contact details of your references, be sure to call (and email) your referees to alert them to expect a call. Tell them about the job you're going for. This will help them sell you when they do receive that call. Referees are valuable and should only be called at the final stage of the job application process.

Recent bosses and people you've worked with for a year or more are good references. Your Mum, cousins, and friends are not good references. If you don't have any references, use a teacher or coach.

Don't ever ask someone to be a reference unless you're sure they'll say something positive about you. Update your referees for each job and advise them when you go for something new.

Length does matter:

Realistically, as a school or uni student your resume should not be more than two pages. If it's more than one page, use page numbers that are the same font but 9 point sized in the footer.

Your resume needs a cover letter:

See Chapter 6 for information on constructing cover letters.

Important resume stuff you need to know...

Fonts:

Always use Arial or Times New Roman. These are the most common business fonts and *if you use a font like this*, be aware that it shows that you have absolutely no idea of how to present yourself professionally. Only use one font and size 12 point throughout your resume.

Fonts *like* this have NO place ON

Things not to do...

- Don't ever use coloured paper
- Don't put 'Resume' or 'Curriculum Vitae' at the top of the page
- Don't make it ridiculously long
- Don't use an email you got when you were twelve (e.g. *Buffy99c@vanillaice.com*)
- Don't use your resume as a place for your comedy routine
- Don't use any photos
- Don't have a coversheet with only your name and address on it
- Don't use a new page for every section
- Don't use clip art cartoons
- Don't use fancy bullet points
- Don't use strange boxes, borders, columns, graphics or tables
- Don't save your resume in a file format people can't open—stick to .doc. A lot of people still, even in 2010, have trouble with .docx and why would you make life harder for someone who may or may not choose you out of a pile of other more accessible applicants?
- Don't use borders or decorations
- Don't ever use snail mail and post your resume—always email. If you <u>do</u> decide to ignore this critical advice, then don't use a binder or a plastic sleeve.

Examples of poorly structured resumes:

Poor Resume Example No. 1:

Hiya, I'd like to be considered for this position. ((my names **tom**._

I'm not that qualifed butI worked at Flexdev. s2 months

For School I went to school at local hihg   School

I am a service extraordinaire small knowledge of OS microsoft word..

Cleaning Duties

1. nice smile :)
2. frendly
3. punctual!
4. Listen to managers rules and follow supervisorâ€™s directions.

Ref: Mrs Tom, m: 0412345678

Call me now on 0412345678.

tommm_mmmazz!@dragonballzmail.com

Gr8 commun1c8er

Poor Resume Example No. 2:

CIRRICULAM VITAE

Tom Winters

E-mail: tommy.winters@gmail.com

Mobile: 0412345678

Career Objective:

   Seeking a technically challenging position in this area providing a highly motivated, progressive, friendly environment, encouraging the pursuit of career advancement and expand my skills and knowledge.

Educational Qualification:

- BA Arts from Macquarie University, Sydney.
-

   Technical Skills:
- Windows NT/2000
- Windows Vista
- Testing Tools
- Core java

Average Resume Example:

Tom Winters

Personal Information

- 31-07-1988
- 12 Principal St, Rockdale 2216
- 02 9512 3456
- 0412 345 678
- tomwinters@gmail.com

Education

2008-Present: Bachelor of Arts at Macquarie University

2002-2007: Sydney Technical High School (UAI 85.72)

Employment History

Jan 2009-Present: Sales Assistant at **Flexible Development Solutions**, Rockdale

My tasks here included:

- Serving customers
- Handling money
- Working as part of a team
- Answering phones

Interests

Rugby League, travel, reading, wine

References available upon request

A Better Resume Example:

Tom Winters

Address: 12 Principal Street,
Rockdale
NSW 2216
Email: tomwinters@gmail.com
H: (02) 9123 4567
M: 0412 345 678

Career Objective:

I am seeking a technically challenging position in a highly motivated, progressive, and friendly environment. I am looking for a position where I can advance my career and expand my skills and knowledge.

Skills:

Sales Skills:
- Assessed customers' needs and recommended products
- Handled customer service issues

Computer Skills:
- Windows NT/2000
- Windows Vista
- Testing tools
- Core Java

Professional Experience:

- **Flexible Development Solutions**
  January 2009: Present, part-time Sales Assistant

Duties and Responsibilities
- Handling money
- Serving Customers
- Working as part of a team

Achievements:

- Employee of the Month, March 2010

Education:

- 2008-present: Bachelor of Arts at Macquarie University
- 2002-2007: Sydney Technical High School (UAI 85.72)

Volunteer Work:

- 2006-2007: Salvation Army Doorknock Appeal

Extra-curricular activities & Interests:

- Rugby League
- Travelling
- Reading

Referees

- Referees will be given upon request

Note: These examples have been applied to small pages. When you create your own resume, you will be able to write in more depth – just don't overdo it!

Show Them What You Got!

This is a list of the top ten *'if you learn nothing else'* tricks that will make your resume stand out!

1. Make it look impressive
2. Use short sentences and bullet points
3. Have big margins (and no borders)
4. Always send by email
5. No more than two pages long
6. Read the job advertisement—why are you right for this job?
7. Correct spelling and grammar
8. Use powerful words like 'implemented', 'changed', 'completed', etc. in your resume
9. Use a little of their industry buzzwords and jargon if you can
10. Call about a week after you send your resume in

So, what's next?

You've done your research, you've sent off your perfect cover letter and resume, so what is the next step? See Chapter 8 to find out!

Chapter 8: Interviews

You have done it! You WOWED them with your resume and now it is time to give the interview that will seal the deal!

All you have to do is go in there and sweep them off their feet. Easy, right?

W e know you've already worked hard to get to this point. Kudos to you for getting here.* But, sadly, your work is not done. Interviews are never as easy as just showing up and taking things as they come. Yes, it is basically a Q&A session, but it's also yet another chance to *sell* yourself. Remember, you will be up against some eager competitors, and if they can sell themselves better, you may miss out on landing your dream job.

So, what can you do to avoid being shown the door?[4]

---

[4] If you have not been offered an interview and can't work out why, go to the end of this chapter and find out exactly <u>where you're going wrong</u> and <u>what you can do about it</u>.

7 Need to know interview facts

1. The ultimate goal of an interview is to **get a job**

2. An interview is a two-way street—a meeting between you and an employer to **find out more about each other**

3. The Scouts' motto is your motto: **'BE PREPARED'**

4. It's OK if you're nervous, just **take slow, deep breaths**

5. The **interviewer is nervous too**, really!

6. You need to **ask them some questions** at the end of the interview

7. Do not make any of the cardinal interview sins!! See below to find out what they are

So, you really want this job?

Preparation is probably the single best thing you can do for your interview. It gets you ahead of the game before you've even stepped into the meeting room. Interviews are a great opportunity that can open the door to your ideal job or to some experience that'll look fantastic on your resume—don't waste an opportunity by thinking it'll go fine if you wing it.

If you are unprepared and it shows, the interviewer will think you have: no motivation, no real interest in the job or company, and no organisational skills. ...**NO CHANCE**

It'll pan out really badly if you don't prepare. We know this because we've seen some fantastic disasters from both the interviewer and interviewee sides of the table. It's no fun for anyone. So, what can you do to prevent this? The answers are easier than you think.

1. Research

The company:

Find out about the company. Who owns it? What are their main products and services? Who are their competitors? This will help you decide if you really want to work for them and it'll also impress your interviewer. A little knowledge can get you pretty far, especially when employers are sadly used to many applicants who don't even know the basic facts of the industry or organisation.

The job:

It's also good to find out some details about the work. If a job description hasn't been provided, ask for one. Or better, speak to someone before the interview with a similar job title. Call the company, ask to speak to the relevant person, and be honest about why you're calling. If you're polite and ask smart questions, chances are they'll be impressed and they'll be telling the person in charge about the call. Remember when the job advertisement said, "showing initiative is critical for success in the role"? Bingo!

The interviewer:

Knowing the name and position of the person who will be interviewing you will do you good, especially if they've got one of those hard-to-pronounce names. Ask the name and title of the person who'll be interviewing you when they schedule the interview time, or call again and inquire if you were too excited to remember to ask.

Think how great an impression it'll make if you turn up and say your interviewer's tricky name correctly as opposed to all the other applicants who butcher it. Assuming that all the applicants are equally qualified (as they generally are, at least on paper), it's little things like this that contribute to the decision of whether you or somebody else gets hired. Use it to your advantage.

7 Interview hints

1. Give a firm handshake (not a knuckle-crusher), and make eye contact when you are first introduced*

2. Natural and relaxed body language is important

3. Smile occasionally, be friendly and pleasant

4. Listen carefully and make sure your replies are to-the-point—don't ramble or be overly dramatic

5. Let them know your qualifications, experience and achievements—sing your own praises

6. Don't talk down your abilities (or over-exaggerate them)

7. Thank the interviewer, express interest, and ask about the next step in the process

*Note: Girls, and especially girls from a migrant background, this means <u>you</u>. However, if you are a practising Muslim woman, and don't shake hands, then explain why.

2. Prepare

Why you?

It is guaranteed that in any interview for any position, your interviewer will be asking about your 'skills and qualities'. Instead of sitting there lost for words, have a think about your strong points **beforehand**. If you were an employer, what would you want to know about a potential employee?

There are a lot of examples from your everyday life where you've shown yourself to be a capable and reliable person. In an interview, use concrete examples that demonstrate a particular skill or personal quality. Maybe you've been promoted? That's music to the ears of employers because it shows them your leadership and interpersonal skills.

Stock questions:

They didn't invite you to their office to socialise. They want to see what kind of person, and potential employee, you are. Be prepared to be asked questions and answer them. Here are a few examples of what they may ask. Practice your answers so if any of these pop up, you're ready to go.

Possible Interview Questions

Tell me about yourself?
This is where you can talk about all the skills and qualities you thought of earlier. Emphasise those that are relevant to the job. If you practice what you want to say beforehand, you don't have to worry that you'll waffle.

What do you expect from this role?
Talk about the invaluable corporate experience you hope to gain. Add your own inputs and thoughts regarding the position on offer.

What attracts you most about our company?
Show off some of the things that you learnt about the company. Knowing the firm's history, market, and core values will show them you've taken the time to do your homework and you're serious about the job.

Why should we hire you?
They're basically saying, "sell yourself to us". Express a genuine interest in the position and relate your skills and experience to their needs.
Give an example of a difficult situation you've had to deal with it and explain how you dealt with it.

They want to see how you handle pressure and whether you're capable of solving problems under stress.

What are some of your strengths and weaknesses?
For strengths, list about two or three and explain how they could benefit the employer. Don't say you don't have any weakness—'nobody's perfect'. Discuss something you may be lacking in and the steps you are taking to combat it.

What do you consider to be your greatest achievement?
They want to know *why* this achievement is important to you and if there are any problems you had to overcome to succeed.

Where do you see yourself in five years?
They want to see your ambitions. Be realistic with your expectations. If you say the Prime Minister, they'll probably think you're being sarcastic.

Big mistake!

"Recently, we interviewed a candidate for a position with our company. I asked him if he had done any research about the company and he told us he hadn't. He followed this up with this great question: 'What is it exactly that your company does?' So not only had he not done any research, but even got our company's name wrong..."—Sean Bailey.

7 Curly questions

1. *Why do you think you're the right candidate for the job?*

It's always hard to think of your strengths on the spot, so try to remember a few that will sell your skills

2. *How would you normally interact within a team?*

They want to know if you delegate, if you piggy-back off others, or if you do your fair share

3. *How would you describe (for example) your education history that's on your resume?*

You may have changed your degree, deferred your studies, left school early, or had short stints at different companies. Prepare an explanation for any of these things. If you stutter through an answer, you're as good as jobless

4. *What three words would your friends use to describe you?*

Nobody is perfect, so you'd be better off listing two good things, and one not-so good thing

5. *Can you mention three or four of our main competitors?*

If you can answer this, it'll score you major 'brownie points'. You get to show them how well informed and interested you are in getting the job

6. *What would you change about your past, if you could?*

This would reveal if you have any regrets or if you're unclear in the direction you want to be heading—see sidenote ***

7. *How do you deal with difficult peers or colleagues?*

This will help the interviewer gauge if you are willing to face internal difficulties and how you solve sticky situations

*** A sidenote from the 'Grey Guru'

"A good answer would have two parts:

"I would not do...again because it kept me from doing/ learning what I really enjoy which is..." Be sure to provide detailed, thoughtful answers to the interview questions, and show the interviewer that you are serious about the job."

There are also the 'unspoken questions' that you need to be aware of.

The interviewer is *really* trying to discover:

- Can you do the job?
- Will you do the job? Is there motivation?
- *Are you the right fit* with the company, the boss, and the rest of the staff?

Be sure to try and convey these things in your answers.

Interviews are a two-way street:

A lot of people go into interviews thinking that it's all about the interviewer and company learning about *them*. **Wrong.**

It all has to do with learning about *each other*. By asking them a few questions, you're showing them that you actually have an interest in the job and the company. Try and avoid asking questions that will make you seem like you didn't prepare enough. The biggest mistake is a shake of the head when they say, "Do you have any questions for us?". Come on, give that interviewer a break—they're tired of doing all the asking. Always have questions for them.

I have some questions for YOU...

1. *What would be the <u>major</u> aspects of my daily job?*

This is your chance to find out more specific on-the-job details, which may not have been advertised or clearly defined. Making sure you know what is expected of you will help indicate whether this role is suitable for you. Remember: the interview is two-sided. It allows the company to find out more about you, but also gives you an insight as to whether the job is right for you!

2. *What kind of <u>mentoring programmes</u> do you offer new graduates/employees?*

The answer to this may show you how the company operates and how much emphasis they put on their graduate employees. It also might make you feel more comfortable and confident in the position you're applying for

3. *How would you describe the <u>culture</u> of the company?*

Your job satisfaction relies heavily on your working environment, so finding out the culture of the company can be very important

4. *What is the <u>team</u> I'll be working with like? What's the structure?*

Just as the culture of the company is important, so is the culture of the team you will be spending your time with. It's a good idea to get some information about these people.

5. *What are some of the <u>career paths</u> potentially available from this position?*

This could help you decide whether this is the most suitable firm for you and whether the position has a long or short term outlook

6. *How many <u>graduates</u> did you hire 2 years ago? What roles are they doing now?*

This will show you how serious and successful the company is about developing their young employees' future careers

7. *What are the <u>next steps</u> after this interview?*

This shows you are proactive and demonstrates your enthusiasm for the role. It also encourages the interviewer to set and give you a definite time frame concerning when you will next be contacted. Knowing their time frame is important (see Ch. 9 for more information on how to follow up interviews)

7 Questions You Should NEVER Ask Your

Interviewer

Never, ever, EVER consider bringing these questions up

1. What product or service do you offer?

They'll know you weren't even bothered to do your research, so how much do you *actually* care about this job?

2. How long will this interview last?

They'll either assume that you think you have something better to do, or you're too disorganised to allow enough time for the interview

3. How much can I expect to be earning?

Unless the interviewer brings this up, never ask. Be comfortable knowing that a quality company will pay a fair salary

4. Do you expect employees to work regular overtime?

This just makes you look lazy, inflexible, and unwilling to put in the extra effort

5. How long does it take to progress in your company?

Ask about career prospects and growth opportunities instead

6. Are there monetary rewards offered for high performance?

They may think money is your main motivation

7. How many days holiday do you offer? How many sick days do you allow?

This will look like all you care about is your time off, not the duties of the job—see sidenote***.

> ### *** A sidenote from the 'Grey Guru'
>
> "You should **never** ask this question. If it's important to you, then perhaps you are more suited to a giant government bureaucracy. It's much better to find out from their website or their employee handouts than asking this during the interview."

So, you've done all the research you possibly could. You've practiced your questions and your answers about a dozen times. There are just a few last minute things you need to do:

Plan your journey in advance. Make sure you know exactly where the place is and how long it'll take you to get there

Leave early enough so that if your train is running late, you'll still get there in time. "Sorry I'm late, I was stuck in traffic," sounds to an interviewer like, "I don't really care about this job". Even if they don't think that specifically, they might simply assume that you don't have very good organisational or time management skills. This is not exactly the impression you want to give when you're asking someone to hire you.

Arriving on time...

> *"When leaving for my first interview with the company I now work for, I was in a rush and ran into a giant, sticky spider web. I then had to run home and clean myself up all over again. Luckily, I was still able to make it to the interview on time. However, feeling rushed/ panicky does not help your nerves before an interview"—Monaz.*

Practice the interview with family and friends to get rid of some of those nerves. Ask them to give you feedback so you can improve. **Have an early night** before the interview. Those bags under your eyes do not scream 'hire me'.

7 Interview mistakes

1. Criticising and talking badly about former employers or colleagues

2. Showing up after 3 hours of sleep, reeking like a distillery. Not only do you need to be 110% on the ball, but hangovers aren't the way to impress interviewers

3. Leaving your mobile on. Don't even leave it on silent— eliminate any chance of embarrassing yourself

4. Talking about personal matters without being asked

5. Bringing along a friend or relative to the interview

6. Chewing gum, smoking (or even smelling like smoke), picking your teeth, whistling, drumming the table, excessively playing with your hair

7. Treating the interviewer and the interview as completely unimportant

An interview horror story...

> *"I once had an interesting experience when a mother dropped off her 20-year-old daughter to an interview. However, she did not just drop her off, but joined her daughter in the actual interview! This is very unprofessional and gives the impression that the 'grown-up' daughter can't make decisions for herself"—Eva.*

Think about your body language...

Your posture, your movements, and expressions portray quite a lot about you. They tell the interviewer if you are nervous, and can provide warning signals if you are lying. Worse, they reveal if you are bored or not paying attention. Watch out for these when you're in an interview:

- **Playing** with your hands
- **Staring** at the interviewer—it's just creepy
- **Slouching** or rocking in your chair
- Having your **arms crossed** over your chest
- **Biting** your nails. Don't even think about cleaning them in front of the interviewer either
- Putting your **hand in front of your mouth** while speaking
- **Leaning** or resting your elbows on the table
- **Gesturing** wildly when you talk. Keep it subtle

Appearance matters!

We'd love to tell you that the interviewer won't make any snap decisions about you the instant that they see you, but that would make us liars. Let's put it this way…

Professional, neat, and conservative appearance says…
"I care about this job."

Baggy, over-revealing, or sloppy appearance says…
"I lack the common sense to try and make a good impression. Don't bother hiring me; I'll only let you down."

7 Interview outfit rules

1. Don't be daring with your outfit

2. Don't over-accessorise. Anything that jangles will only annoy the interviewer

3. Don't show up with your piercings in. Nose studs, tongue rings, and eyebrow rings are not welcome

4. Don't bathe yourself in perfume or aftershave. Make-up should be subtle too

5. Do wear the best suit or work attire you can find. If you don't have anything that fits this mould, borrow from someone you know

6. Do shine your **shoes** and make sure your clothes are wrinkle and lint-free

7. Do clean and trim your nails. The night before your interview is not the time to try out the fluoro-pink nail polish

We know you're nervous, but it's always a good idea to come across as happy, friendly, and polite. When employers decide who they are going to hire, it may simply boil down to who they liked the best—who they had great chemistry with, and not necessarily the person who had the best skills, experience or exam results.

What to expect when you step into the room...

Like we said, interviews are a bit more than a Q&A session. They can take different forms, and it'll help your chances if you know if it's a first-round interview or a one-off panel interview. It's also a good thing to know how long the interview may take. There would be nothing worse than having to cut off the interviewer telling them you've got to run to that doctor's appointment.

A general structure: Regardless of the type of interview, the interviewer will always follow the same pattern. First, there are the preliminary questions, where there'll be a bit of small talk to warm you up and put you at ease.

7 Small talk topics

1. The weather. Yes, it may be a boring one, but it gets the ball rolling
2. A little bit about you
3. How easily you found the office
4. Hobbies or interests on your resume
5. What you like to do in your spare time
6. How much you enjoy going to your university and the subjects you take
7. First impressions of the place

Then they get into the nitty-gritty stuff. The critical questioning time is used when the interviewer wants to get all the information they can to assess your skills.

Next is where you come in with your questions. It's a vital part of the process, so don't throw your chance away by not asking anything.

Before you know it, you're shaking their hand and asking about the next stage and when you'll be hearing from them.

Note: Beware of the danger points—the <u>beginning</u> and <u>end</u> of an interview. People always relax and let their guard down at the beginning, or when the interview is over. Some interviewers may make a point of walking you to the lift, or even going down to the lobby with you. People are at the most revealing when they think the formal interview is over. The interview is only truly over when you've left the building. Sometimes, there are receptionists who may have been asked to do a little spying on you.

Another interview disaster…

> *"I once interviewed a candidate for an Accounting position. This was when our agency shared a large office and a reception with two other firms. After the interview had finished up, the applicant caught the lift down with a receptionist from one of the other firms and phoned his friend. The receptionist overheard this conversation, with the applicant saying that he thought he totally aced the interview even though he admitted to having no clue what work the position entailed, or what specific work the company did. Of course, this information got back to me and our agency consequently rejected this applicant"—Sean Bailey.*

It is also worth pointing out that different employers use different methods to get the goods on their applicants, so let's look at a few different ways the interview may be conducted.

Assessment centres or **small-scale** testing is quite common, especially with those big organisations that offer graduate programmes and summer internships. They use these to see how candidates encounter, handle, and perform in both individual and group-based exercises, and simulated work scenarios. There could be case studies, practical exercises to test your knowledge of computer programmes, spelling and grammar quizzes, or even aptitude tests.

7 Tips on how NOT to deal with a group situation

1. Dominate the conversation
2. Be too shy and let the other applicants get all the attention
3. Interrupt others. It doesn't scream "I work well in teams"
4. Speaking in the third-person. People may think you're pretentious
5. Putting others down. Remember, no badmouthing previous employers
6. Forgetting the other group members' names. It shows that you are inattentive, and forgetful
7. No name-dropping

Two Different Types of Interviews:

The **informational interview** is a one-on-one session where the interviewer gathers information to get to know you and your skills better, and where you can learn more about the organisation. In this sort of interview, you could ask them something like:

"What skills are essential to do this job well?"

The **behavioural** or **situational** interview focuses on your past experiences, and uses them to try and predict future behaviours. This is when you have to use specific examples of your abilities and experience. There's usually a standard format of:

What was the situation?
What was your action?
What was the outcome?

They could ask you questions like...

- *Describe one of the biggest responsibilities you've had in the past and how you managed it.*

- *What different approaches do you take in talking to people of a different status? Give an example and explain the outcome.*

- *Describe a time when you had to make an important decision within the last year?*

- *Can you give an example of a time when you demonstrated close attention to detail?*

- *Have you ever come up with ways to make a job you were doing easier?*

Phone interviews are usually the first stage in the interviewing process between you and a potential employer. Phone interviews give employers a chance to get a feel for the way you think, speak and handle pressure. It may be harder to get your point across so make sure you are clear, articulate, and speaking at a pace slower than a horseracing commentator.

7 Best phone interview tips

1. Be prepared for the call. If you're out or not prepared, ask them when would be an appropriate time to call them back

2. Have relevant information handy. Write down your strengths and weaknesses, availabilities, and questions you want to ask the interviewer

3. Have a copy of your resume in front of you

4. Use a quiet room and have a pen and notepad, calendar, and the job advertisement in front of you

5. Try to do the interview over a landline

6. Be confident and clear. They're judging your verbal communication skills , so try not to mumble and waffle

7. Think before you speak. Don't feel like you need to say the first thing that comes to mind. Gather your thoughts and answer the question

What not to do in a phone interview...

"I once had a phone interviewee who would not stop talking! She did show potential for the position, but struggled to focus on the questions at hand, consequently the interview lasted for half an hour. She didn't make it to the second round..."—Monaz.

Sometimes, employers want a range of evaluations of an interviewee, so they'll use a **panel** of interviewers. When answering questions, focus on the person who asked it but don't exclude the other panel members. Be sure to interact with all of them.

7 Things you must do in an interview

If you forget everything else, remember these ways to win the interviewer's stamp of approval

1. Your handshake must be firm. Remember to make eye contact

2. Be natural and (appear) relaxed. Smile every now and then, and show them how friendly and enthusiastic you are

3. Don't start off using their first name. A surname will do unless they say, "Oh please, call me Sandy"

4. Be brief and to the point. Don't ramble or be dramatic

5. Listen carefully. There's nothing more embarrassing than not being able to answer a question because you were too busy day dreaming about lunch

6. Emphasise your qualifications, experience, strengths and achievements. Boast a little, just don't exaggerate

7. Thank the interviewer, express your interest, and ask about the next stage. If you don't do this, they may think you're not that interested

Not getting called back for interviews?

If you're not getting selected for interviews, consider the following:

- Are you qualified enough for this role? Is the position suitable for a recent graduate? Don't waste your time by applying for the wrong positions

- Are you tailoring your applications to particular positions?

- Do you show that you understand what the job involves?

- Do you address the selection criteria, including relevant experience, skills and knowledge?

- Have you highlighted all your job-related skills and qualities?

- Is your resume professional and well presented?

- Does your cover letter sell you? Is the tone appropriate?

- Has your application been carefully proofread? Ask a friend or family member to do this for you

Shaken those nerves yet?

The interview process is over—or is it? Read Chapter 9 to find out what you have to do after the initial interview to secure your dream job.

Chapter 9: Interview Follow up

Your work is still not done. Be above average: follow up on that interview!

You're so close that you can practically taste that dream job. Now is <u>not</u> the time to sit by and watch someone else get it.

Y ou beat those nerves, asked the interviewers killer questions, and charmed the pants off them with your winning smile. The decision is now in their hands, all you have to do is wait.

Except that would be, without a doubt, the wrong attitude to have.

It's a common mistake of job applicants to think that once the interview is over, it is all out of their control. They think that they've done all that they possibly can—they fall back on fate to decide their future.

What many fail to realise is that there *is* another chance for them to prove their commitment and enthusiasm. There is one more way to push yourself ahead of the competition. It's so simple! So, what can you do to get ahead of the game? Follow up after the interview.

Follow up strategy 1:

The email:

It all starts with a 'thank you' email. If you've decided you still want the job after the interview, there's no better way to build a relationship with the interviewer and the company than by just saying a small thank you. A *short* thank you tells them that you're still interested in the position and appreciate their interest in you.

7 Tips for your thank you email

1. Get the business card of your interviewer on your way out of the interview. That way you have their email address and the right spelling of their name

2. Write individual 'thank you' emails if there was more than one interviewer. They can be more or less the same, but make sure to personalise them a little

3. Show your appreciation for their time and interest in you

4. Remind them that you are a fantastic candidate

5. If you can, include some more information about yourself that they may find useful in making their decision

6. Send your 'thank you' email about two business days after the interview

7. As with everything else, proofread your letter. Grammar or spelling mistakes may put you in the 'No Thanks' pile

The Thank You Email Template

Dear Mr. /Ms. Last name:

Use this paragraph to thank the interviewer for taking the time to meet with you. Remember to say how interested you are in the position.

The second paragraph is where you'd put all the reasons why you are a great candidate. Don't forget to match your skills to their job.

This paragraph is optional and is where you'd mention anything you forgot to bring up in the interview that you think they should know— especially if it was something you *should* have said.

The closing paragraph tells the interviewer you look forward to hearing from them soon.

Sincerely,

And type your name here

Try something like...

Good morning, Mr. Smith,

Thank you again for your time on Wednesday. I really enjoyed the interview and would like to restate my interest in the position. Please call or email me if there are any updates about the job.

Sincerely,

Tom Winters

Or

Dear Mr. Smith,

Thank you again for your time on Wednesday. I really enjoyed the interview and would like to restate my interest in the position.

After listening to what you had to say about the company, I really believe I would be a strong candidate for the position. I offer the flexibility and dependability that is required of the job and believe that I can learn a lot from your company.

In addition to my enthusiasm for the role, I would also bring a high level of organisational and communication skills.

I am very interested in this job, and look forward to hearing from you soon. Please email or call me on 0401 023 345 if there are any updates about this position.

Sincerely,

Tom Winters

You can change your letter in small ways to suit your purpose. If you want to stress how well you'd fit in with the organisation, tell them that you enjoyed getting to know more about their company/business during the interview, and feel that you will get along well with other team members. Or maybe you thought of something after the interview that you **need** them to know? Make sure your 'thank you' email includes each of these key points:

"I forgot to mention during the interview that…"

"I wanted to make sure that you knew…"

Keep your email short and to-the-point. It is <u>just</u> an email saying thank you, not an essay.

Follow up strategy 2:

The phone call:

When leaving the interview, it's a good idea to ask the interviewers when you can expect to hear from them. Don't freak out if you don't hear back from them on that day as there could be several reasons why they haven't called you yet. Wait two or three business days after they said they'd call, and then give <u>them</u> a call.

Note: Don't sound too desperate or needy. Let them know you're still interested in the position and ask if there's any other information they need from you. If this doesn't get them to give you some feedback about the position, ask for a specific date to call again and get feedback.

Try something like:

I just wanted to thank you again for your time on Wednesday. I'm still very interested in the position, and was wondering if there were any updates on my application.

If the interviewer is unavailable, make sure to leave a message for them, either through a voicemail, or with their secretary. Be sure to say your name slowly and clearly.

7 Important Phone Call No-No's

(Avoid these at all costs!)

1. Making contact if they specifically said after the interview not to. Wait for the interviewers to get back to you, but do ask when you can expect to hear from them

2. Calling more than once a week or earlier than the date they said they'd call. You may appear too desperate

3. Telling them you'll take any position other than the one you were interviewed for

4. Letting them think that this particular position is your only option—see sidenote ***

5. Constantly calling them after they haven't returned your calls.

6. Asking if there's anything you can tell them that will convince them to hire you

7. Overstepping boundaries and becoming a nuisance

***A sidenote from the *'Grey Guru'*

"I've applied for other jobs. Do I tell them? Will it help my chances?"

"Use other job offers to get some leverage, but <u>very carefully.</u> If you are too obvious or aggressive, many employers may decide that they don't want someone like you on their team*. This is problematic if your motive is just to get more money. A good way to leverage when you want the job is to let them know you have another offer(s), but that you are really interested in *their* company/business and learning more about it. It's likely that if they know other companies are interested in you, they will 'upgrade' your application; they wouldn't want a competitor to snatch something good from them. Of course you wouldn't mention <u>who</u> has made you an offer unless you want them to question your discretion. Quite rightly, they'll wonder if you're touting <u>their</u> name around the market as well."

"***Note**: Investment banks were perhaps an exception until 2008. Many of their interviewers would see this as gutsy or proof that they would 'take no prisoners', that they would thrive in the tough world of doing deals. Their so-called toughness didn't survive when the markets got tough; investment banks have nearly all gone broke."

Not hearing from them on the day they said they'd get back to you doesn't mean that you missed out, so don't let it get to you. We know it's nerve-wracking and you can't help but overanalyse every little thing you did and said in the interview to try to pinpoint what you could have done better. Sometimes, it's simply not about you.

The hiring process can often take longer than you would like it to. Scheduling conflicts can delay interviews, and there can be a lot of paperwork and red tape involved in finalising decisions regarding employment. Sometimes it's just a case of bad organisation on their part. So basically, it's not your fault. Reassuring, isn't it?

Wait the two or three days we suggested, and after expressing your interest, politely ask if they have an idea of a timeline, or when they'll be making a decision.

While you are waiting...

So you feel like the interview went great? You sent your 'thank you' email and/or made the necessary phone calls. Surely you've snagged your dream job. Don't forget that nothing's certain until they've actually *offered* you the position. It really is true that it's better to be safe than sorry, so you should keep looking for jobs, applying for them, and participating in interviews. It's happened on way too many occasions that someone's been convinced that they scored the job, only to be rejected with no other job options. It's in your best interests to continue job-hunting as if no interview ever took place.

When you don't get the offer...

Sometimes, things don't work out as you'd like them to. Firstly, don't let the knockbacks get to you too much. Remember, you weren't the *only* applicant to be rejected. We know it's not easy being turned down, but try not to burn any bridges. You never know what may come up in the future, or who the interviewer can put you in touch with.

Also, keep in mind that not all companies will be the right fit for you. Interviews are kind of like a blind date—you need to go and investigate the situation, and see if there's chemistry between you and the company, or if you're just hearing crickets. If it's the latter, you need to get back on the horse and keep looking for that ideal job. Don't put too much importance on any one job or interview; there *will* be others, so think of each interview as practice.

One of the best things you can do with rejection is to get some **feedback**. There could have been dozens of reasons that could have affected your chances, so it's a good idea to see what your shortcomings were. That way you can work on them for the next interview.

Maybe it was your appearance, or possibly that you knew too little about the company. Perhaps your questions were totally irrelevant. You'll never know unless you call and ask them.

7 Ways to deal with feedback

1. Don't let them know you're unhappy with being unsuccessful
2. Try and stay positive when making the phone call
3. Don't take the rejection personally— see sidenote ***
4. Don't act defensively or the interviewer won't be able to give you any useful feedback
5. Show that you understand the reasons why you didn't get the job and ask what you could have done better

6. Don't use the phone call as an opportunity to argue and persuade them to hire you. Trust us, it will not help your case
7. Don't get discouraged. There is a job out there for you— you just have to find it

***A sidenote from the 'Grey Guru'

A salesman who is really good at making cold calls knows that on average they have to make 20 calls to get just the one sale. Treat each rejection as a _good_ thing; you are now one step closer to the sale. Of course, really great salespeople don't make cold calls. Just as _you don't_ submit cold, un-targetable, un-researched job applications. Nor do you wander around a job fair randomly picking up brochures like 99% of your fellow students—this is just a waste of time."

All your hard work has paid off!

So you have put in all the hard work, and you have finally been rewarded. Read Chapter 10 to find out what to do next

Chapter 10: Dream Jobs

Landing your DREAM job

All that work you put in has finally paid off. Your fantastic cover letter, that unreal resume, the killer interview—you have been offered your dream job.

Your immediate reaction may be to accept the position on the spot, especially if it's the first offer you've received for a 'real' job. However, sometimes it's a good idea to take a step back and look at the bigger picture.

Is this what I really want?

Take the time to consider your options. Whether they made the offer over the phone or in writing, ask if you can have a few days to decide. It is <u>highly</u> unlikely that you'll lose the position by doing this; they won't go and give the job to their second choice. In fact, it may even make you seem more valuable. People always want what's harder to attain and by asking for some time, you've just made yourself that much more appealing.

7 Things to consider

1. Your job description and duties
2. The culture of the workplace
3. The company's view on study leave or funding study courses
4. What opportunities there are for promotions or further training

5. Salary and extra benefits—see sidenote ***
6. Are the company's values compatible with yours?
7. Travel time to and from work

*** A sidenote from the 'Grey Guru'

"If you're making a choice between two job offers, don't make the decision based solely on salary. Many graduates have found that those very enticing salaries also come with roles that are way too demanding or are really boring. Sometimes they pay high salaries because the company and the job are just awful!"

If some things are a bit unclear, call them back and ask for more information. You may discover something new about the position or about how they work together at the office that will help you make your decision. It will also give them the impression that you're considering the offer in a professional way.

It's likely that they would have given you up until a certain date to make your decision, so it's important you find out all the facts as soon as you can.

It doesn't rain, it pours...

You may have been lucky enough to have received more than one job offer. You need to weigh up the advantages and disadvantages of each position, and how they fit into your plans for your future. Don't just look at the short-term, think about the long-term benefits of taking a certain position. More importantly, don't choose one job over another just because of the salary.

If you've been offered a position with one company, but you're still waiting to hear back from another, you may want to contact both companies. Contact the first company to figure out how long until you have to make a decision, and the second to see if they're any closer to making a decision. If the second company is interested in hiring you, knowing that you already have an offer, it may encourage them to speed up their decision-making.

When the job just doesn't fit...

Sometimes that job isn't your ideal choice for a career. There's nothing wrong with wanting to decline a job offer as you have no obligation to accept it. Wouldn't you rather be happy in the *right* job than just take any job for the sake of it?

7 Warning signs to look out for

1. Feedback is minimal and does not provide enough information

2. The job description is unclear

3. You haven't met your future boss or co-workers

4. The job doesn't allow you to learn new skills

5. There is little emphasis on training

6. The company is under financial pressure

7. You're not sure what you have to do to perform well

Accepting an offer...

As soon as you've decided to accept an offer, be sure to do so in writing. If you get any other offers once you've accepted, it would be in your best interests to politely decline. Many employers are in contact with one another, and you never know what, or who, may come up in their conversations. It'll reflect badly on you and may hurt your chances in future job searches.

Rejecting an offer...

When rejecting job offers, make sure you're professional, polite and tactful.

When you need to resign...

If you're already employed when offered a new job, you're going to have to resign from your current position. Similar to when you decline a job offer, when resigning, you need to do so in a polite and formal manner. It's a good idea to do it in writing.

How to resign the right way...

- Tell them you have accepted and signed a job offer and that you are resigning, effective immediately.
- Hand them a signed letter of resignation
- Thank them for the opportunity to work there and express regret that you're leaving
- Offer to help them in a way that will minimise disruption from your leaving

The most important thing about your letter of resignation is to get it to your manager and to Human Resources as soon as you've made your decision. That way, there's no doubt about your date of resignation and no confusion over how much notice you've given. Be as professional and polite as possible; you never know when you may need help from your colleagues in the future.

Glossary of Australian terms...

ATAR: The Australian Tertiary Admission Rank. This recently implemented system replaces the University Admissions Index (UAI) and serves as the primary determinant for a person's entry into a university undergraduate program.

TAFE: Technical and Further Education. TAFE is a tertiary education institution that focuses on vocational education and training, providing a different learning experience to that of university. The duration of a TAFE course ranges from six months to two years and concentrates on industry developed learning and practical work experience. Differing from university Bachelor degree programs, upon completion of a TAFE course, graduates can receive qualifications including Certificates, Diplomas and Advanced Diplomas.

UAI: University Admissions Index. A UAI is an index calculated for New South Wales Higher School Certificate graduates which is used to determine their eligibility for admission into university undergraduate courses.